IN THE SHADOW OF A GIANT

MEL CHARLES
WITH COLIN LESLIE

IN THE SHADOW OF A GIANT

THE AUTOBIOGRAPHY OF ARSENAL AND WALES LEGEND

JOHN BLAKE

Published by John Blake Publishing Ltd,
3 Bramber Court, 2 Bramber Road,
London W14 9PB, England

www.johnblakepublishing.co.uk

First published in hardback in 2009

ISBN: 978-1-84454-776-0

British Library Cataloguing-in-Publication Data:

A catalogue record for this book is available from the British Library.

Design by www.envydesign.co.uk

Printed in the UK by CPI William Clowes Beccles NR34 7TL

1 3 5 7 9 10 8 6 4 2

Papers used by John Blake Publishing are natural, recyclable products made
from wood grown in sustainable forests. The manufacturing processes conform
to the environmental regulations of the country of origin.

To Jeremy, Catherine, Lauryn, Michael
and the memory of John.

CONTENTS

ACKNOWLEDGEMENTS

Thanks to Jack Charlton and John Toshack for their kind forewords; Michelle Signore, Victoria McGeown, Allie Collins and all the staff at John Blake; Gareth Vincent and Steve Phillips at the South Wales Evening Post; Dafydd Wyn Jones, Gerallt Owen and Gareth Williams at Porthmadog; Kevin Bryce at Haverfordwest; Iain Cook at Arsenal; Ceri Stennett at the Football Association of Wales; Tony Woolway and Saffron Herbert at Media Wales; Jonathan Wilsher at Swansea City FC; Richard Shepherd at Cardiff City FC; Cliff Jones, Terry Medwin, Mel Nurse, David Farmer; Neil Markham, Stuart and Sally Hall for their help with proof-reading; Gerard Morris and Paul Dicks; the regulars at the Badminton Bar, Sandfields, Swansea; Mario Risoli for providing the inspiration with his books on John Charles and Wales at the 1958 World Cup; Swansea Libraries; S.E.A; Donald Walker for his support; Richard Moore and Stan for their early advice; Kenny Darling and Pete Mason for their help sourcing pictures; and John Weaver for his imaginative book title.

FOREWORD

BY JOHN TOSHACK AND
JACK CHARLTON

Has there ever been such a footballing family as famous as the Charles family? I don't think so. I have to say that John was my absolute idol when I started as a schoolboy but I was also aware of his brother, Mel. Mel was, I thought, a super centre-half. I maintain that was his best position, and irrespective of big brother John's fame, I'm sure Mel would have been a real star in his own right. Mel's son Jeremy later played for me at Swansea and, like father Mel and uncle John, he was a full Welsh international.

I suppose it is inevitable that when talking about Mel we have to refer to his brother John as well. I'm sure Mel is used to that by now and I'm even more sure that he doesn't mind in the slightest. I'm just pleased and privileged to have known them both and I know what I'm talking about when I say that John was the greatest, but don't underestimate Mel either. I would always have had him in my team! Good luck.

John Toshack

Melvyn and I were very close as teenagers, when we were on the groundstaff at Leeds United – cleaning toilets, sweeping the stands, weeding the pitch – all for less than a fiver a week. He would come up to my home at Ashington some weekends and meet my brother Bobby and the rest of my family. I remember waving him off at the train station as he went off on what was meant to be a trip home – except he never came back. I was so sorry to see him go – he was a good friend and quite a character. But he had got homesick and decided to stay in his home town, Swansea. The rest is history. The next time I saw him I was playing against him for England against Wales in an international match, but it was a friendship which lasted throughout our careers as our paths crossed for club and country.

Mel was an excellent player and he did well at the World Cup in Sweden in 1958. I was glad to see him get his big break with Arsenal, but any mention of Melvyn was inevitably followed by a mention of his big brother John, a giant of a man and a giant of a footballer. He was a different class and the best header of a ball I ever saw; he was older than me, and a big influence on all around him at Leeds, and occasionally he would take me aside and teach me some of his techniques. Like Melvyn, he was a great guy. I have been asked many times to name my best team of all time, and I can honestly say John Charles would be the first name on my team sheet.

People talk about Bobby and me – the Charlton brothers – and our place in British football history, but the Charles brothers should be right there alongside us. They were two fantastic players who I have been proud to know.

Jack Charlton

CHAPTER 1
LOOKING UP TO A GIANT

'John Charles wasn't only one of the greatest footballers who ever lived. He was one of the greatest men ever to have played the game.'
SIR BOBBY ROBSON

BEING THE BROTHER of John Charles, the most famous sportsman Wales has ever produced and maybe the best all-round footballer Britain has ever seen, was never going to be easy. John – the Gentle Giant, or *Il Gigante Buono* as his adoring fans at Juventus christened him – was the greatest, and how do you follow that? The answer is that you can't.

Not that I have a single regret about my career, life or being John's brother – I'm proud on all three counts. I've had a hell of a life and never a day goes by when I'm not grateful for the experiences I had as a player with Swansea Town, Cardiff City, Arsenal and Wales, then in the twilight years of my career with Port Vale and Welsh League sides Porthmadog and Haverfordwest County when I was playing mainly for beer money. We didn't do too badly between us, John and me really, from two dirty-faced little kids playing football in the park during our humble working-class upbringing in Cwmbwrla, Swansea, to international footballers travelling the world and seeing exotic places like Brazil, Mexico and Mauritius. But whatever I did, I was always going to be in the shadow of big John, who at the peak of his powers with Juventus was the best footballer in the world – the superstar of his generation.

Funnily enough, although we were brothers and we were very close as we grew up, we didn't see much of each other during our playing careers. Neither of us had been bright academically, maybe because most of our brains were in our feet, so when we left school we were barely able to read or write. Because of that, it didn't make it easy to stay in touch, and we just got on with our own lives. So John just went his way, all the way to Italy as it turned out, and I went mine, and the only time we would really see each other was when we joined up with the Wales squad for internationals. There was no big fuss, just a smile and a handshake like we had seen each other the day before, but we always got on well. We understood each other, knew each other inside out, and our personalities seemed to fit together very well. John was far quieter than me mind you; I was the wayward one, although that's not to say he was an angel, far from it. He always behaved impeccably on the pitch though and he was an inspiration to those in his team and the thousands that watched him in awe and admiration from the terraces.

As a player, John had everything in his locker – great timing, balance, skill and poise, and he was a colossus in the air. He was six foot two and built like an Adonis, but never once did he use that physique to bully or intimidate; he always channelled his attributes and his power in the right way. They were gifts and he used them wisely. Whoever coined the name 'Gentle Giant' was a genius because it fitted John like a glove. If he cut an impressive figure on the outside, then it was mirrored on the inside too. He was a lovely bloke, as I am sure anybody who met him will agree, and to be his brother always did, and still does, make me very proud.

We were both privileged enough to play our way through what can now be looked back on as a truly golden era for Welsh football, and he was at the core of that great international team. For two boys from Cwmbwrla to be lining up against the best of the world, including the greatest of all-time Pelé, was something way beyond our wildest dreams as we grew up with barely two pennies to rub together during the War. But the Charles brothers had the honour of representing Wales at the 1958 World Cup, the one and only time our nation has made it to the finals, and while I live in hope that the team of today might one day emulate our team, it is a distinction that I treasure.

There were quite a few footballing brothers back in the Fifties and Sixties, but it was nice to be one half of one of the most famous sets. We shared some great times together wearing the red shirt of Wales, and while there was no doubt a few times that John shook his head and worried about his slightly wilder younger brother, the worst he would do was take me aside and do his best to keep me on the straight and narrow. He would never try to throw his weight about and I think he took a lot of pride in the fact that I was, to a degree, following in his footsteps and also that we were getting to live these great experiences together. It still warms my heart to this day when people come up and want to shake your hand, say that they saw you play in your heyday, and thank you for any happy memories that you have provided them with.

But people couldn't help comparing us, with me forever the one following in John's impressive shadow. I followed him up to Leeds United after leaving school, then on to the ground staff of Swansea Town and of course alongside him into the Wales side, and wherever I went, I found that the comparisons would swiftly be made between the two Charles brothers. Even when I signed for Arsenal, I was quickly judged in relation to whatever John was doing with Juventus in Italy – and he was usually doing superbly well. He was the yardstick by which I was measured. But while it might have been human nature to bracket the two brothers together and make snap judgments, it was no good doing that because we were different players, different people, and it could be frustrating when some people had difficulty in making the distinction.

Some people think I was as good as John, while others do not, but I didn't ever envy what John achieved – I never did. I think most people who say that I was as good are the older Swansea fans, who saw me play some of the best football of my career at the Vetch Field but were deprived of seeing John wear the white shirt of his home-town club. Fate took him away as a teenager before he had played a game, never to return to the club. I think people in Swansea still wonder what might have been had his career path not taken him to Leeds at that early age, but if they are being honest it would only have been a matter of time before a big club came in and spirited away one of their favourite sons.

I was always so proud of what he did in his career. The upbringing we had left no room for jealousy. We were taught to be happy with our lot and to stick by our family through thick and thin, and I only took pride in what John did throughout his life. He had his ups and downs like I did and made a few decisions he would regret, but I always stuck by him and so did the rest of my family. He was my big hero and I'm just proud to be his brother. If I liked it or not though, I did find that I always had to live up to my brother's name, and when my son Jeremy went on to make it as a footballer too, playing for Swansea City, Queens Park Rangers and Oxford, and following in our footsteps by winning caps for Wales, he too had to live up to the name of me and John – the family honour was always hanging round our necks and it wasn't always an easy burden to carry. John was a great big star of that era, a trailblazer and an ambassador for British football, and I was coming up behind him, trying to negotiate a path for my own career. But I could never be like him, could I?

Have a look at his career statistics and you'll see what I mean. He scored an amazing 93 goals in 155 matches for Juventus and was the top goalscorer in Serie A, making him a star the world over. I remember once going over to visit him in Italy. The club catered for his every need and he stayed in a beautiful house overlooking Lake Como. He wore beautiful tailored Italian suits, drove a handsome big car and could not go anywhere in Turin without being hailed as a hero by a passer-by or invited into a restaurant. He also mixed with the rich and famous in Italy and on this one occasion when I went over, he told me that he had been invited to Sophia Loren's party and asked me if I fancied coming along. Before my jaw hit the ground, I told him I would be there all right. While I was glad to be going over to see big John and spend some quality time with him, all of a sudden the real highlight of the trip to Italy was going to be that party and living *la dolce vita* by spending some time in the presence of one of the most beautiful film stars in the world at a high-society gathering.

I had trouble keeping the butterflies at bay after getting that dream party invite and envisioned having a good old chinwag with the hostess, but when it came to the night of the party John wasn't feeling too chipper and to my absolute horror said that he couldn't be bothered and didn't fancy going anymore. Can you believe it? Sophia Loren's bash and you can't be bothered? There was barely a man alive on the planet at that time who would have passed on that one, but John did. I had a real go at him for that, I was absolutely gutted, and couldn't just gatecrash the party myself. It was John Charles who opened doors for you in those circles, and they probably hadn't even heard of me. I suppose that was one of the few times, other than when I was a kid, that I lost my rag with John. I had bought a suit especially for the occasion, a nice white one which would have been a knock-out, but instead it sat hanging in a wardrobe gathering mothballs for years and whenever I looked at it, I would remember how big John had deprived me of the chance to see Sophia Loren. It didn't take me long to forgive him though, any cross words that we had were always quickly forgotten and moments later we were best friends again. That's just the way we were, both big easy-going chaps and we always hit it off and brought out the best in each other.

When John moved to Juventus from Leeds United in 1957 he went for what was then a world record transfer of £65,000. In his first spell at Leeds he scored 150 goals in 297 matches, and then he quickly established himself as a legend in what was the hardest and richest league in the world. He also proved himself a worldwide star at international level, winning 38 caps for Wales and scoring 15 goals. Wherever Wales would play, it was John Charles the opposition fans and players would be looking out for. He would have won a lot more caps for Wales too had it not been for the constant tug-of-war that would develop between club and country whenever an international came around while he was a Juventus player.

I suppose John's real talent was that he was the complete footballer. He wasn't just a player who was brilliant as a defender or brilliant as an attacker, you could stick him anywhere and he would be brilliant. He could breeze through a game at centre-half or at centre-forward, and even when he was playing at the back he was a constant goal threat. His heading ability was phenomenal. Even the Queen knew who John Charles was – she awarded him the CBE at Buckingham Palace – not bad going for a lad from Cwmbwrla.

With a career like that to follow, I do feel that being John's brother always overshadowed what I did as a player, and there's never been any getting away from that. John was such a star and such a famous fellow, and I think I felt that a lot of people expected me to be just as good or even better in time because I was three-and-a-half years younger than him. I was also the spitting image of him, even if he was a bit bigger than me. If John was scoring X amount of goals, they immediately expected me to do the same. And because John was the highest goalscorer over in Italy, in Serie A, they expected me to be the highest goalscorer here, in the English First Division. While I had always found that I was expected to live up to his name, the pressure multiplied the moment I pulled on an Arsenal shirt. I had been bought for a British record transfer fee, and while I wasn't John Charles, I think a lot of fans, journalists and observers thought I would be the next best thing. Anything less would be deemed a failure and that weight of expectation would dog me during my years at Highbury. That kind of pressure can be the worst thing ever in terms of trying to keep your career on track, but looking back I can see clearly now that it was never going to be easy having a brother as famous as John. In many respects I suppose it's like the Charlton brothers, isn't it? Bobby was the one who got all the headlines, broke all the records and scored all the goals, while Jackie was just regarded as the stalwart at the back. Bobby was always regarded as the number one, and it was the same with John. But I didn't ever worry about that because I knew more than anybody else what John was like as a person and a player – great in every respect. He was not an easy act to follow, but that's life I suppose.

I have an old football annual in the house, printed not long after the World Cup in 1958 and my then-British record transfer from Swansea Town to Arsenal in 1959, where our respective careers and ability were examined in close detail. The article was headed JOHN AND MEL – TWO KINGS OF SOCCER and it says:

'The Charles brothers are well worth the fabulous fees paid for their services. With the transfer of Mel to Arsenal for something over £40,000, there has been considerable discussion about which is the better footballer. But when a player is as good as either of the Charles brothers it hardly matters which is the better. Any difference at that level of attainment can only be slight and relative (no pun intended). But it might be interesting to learn the opinions of two people who are well qualified, and most experienced judges of the game.

Jimmy Murphy, the Welsh national team manager and assistant to Matt Busby at Manchester United, for instance: "I would say Mel is not such a good all-round man as his brother. In my opinion, John has the greater natural ability." On the other hand, Murphy states: "Mel was one of our few outstanding successes in Sweden, where he played five games at centre-half."

'Willy Meisl, the Austrian who has become a top British soccer writer, says: *"I would rank Mel above his brother at the moment. Although John is the more valuable as forward, he does not compare with Mel at half-back. In Sweden last summer, Mel not only shared with goalkeeper Jack Kelsey the honour of being the best player in the World Cup but was one of the best dozen players in the whole tournament."'*

The article adds: *'John has better club facilities and conditions than Mel will get even at Highbury. Is it any wonder that "Big John" went to Italy? Whether or not he is a slightly better player than Mel does not matter, as it is pretty well agreed that they are both in the five top players in British football. John does not shirk work, even though it is harder for him than most because he is naturally inclined to be a bit lazy. So is brother Mel – he is also a little more carefree and casual about life than John. It is natural that, being brothers, their careers should have followed broadly similar patterns, but at times the similarity has stretched coincidence almost to the point of incredibility.'*

I think that article, written nearly 50 years ago, sums up nicely how John and I were always bracketed together, but so far as the debate goes as to who was the better player, let me have the casting vote... it was John. We were different players, and I was proud of a lot that I achieved in my career, but signing for Arsenal and the knee problems that I developed while I was there probably stopped me fulfilling my full potential, while John's achievements with Juventus were nothing short of amazing. He was the greatest, and if I'm even going to be mentioned in the same breath as him, I am happy to settle for that.

With John going back and forth to Italy like a yo-yo, from Leeds to Juventus, then Juventus to Leeds, then Leeds to Roma, we spent large chunks of time apart. But we finally got our chance to play in the same club side when he came home to sign for Cardiff City, the club I had joined after my injury-hit time at Arsenal. There proved to be a few ups and downs on the pitch, but it was time together that we hugely valued. When we were apart as players we didn't really keep in touch – we would just meet up whenever there was an international or during the close season. We were very, very close though, no doubt about it, but when he was away we just had to get on with things – we had our own lives and playing careers. As well as the ill-fated trip out for the Sophia Loren party, I travelled to Italy to see him a few times, whenever the chance arose, and I would go up to see him in Leeds quite a lot when he settled up there after we'd both hung up the boots. We always enjoyed one another's company after our football careers had finished in the mid-Seventies, from one or two hair-brained Kamikaze business schemes that we embarked upon to the many charity and exhibition matches that we played in alongside Jeremy, Sir Stanley Matthews and quite a few of our old Wales mates, to the more relaxed times as we grew old and grey.

The death of John in 2004 hit me hard, as it did the whole of Wales. He had been a living legend in his homeland, and I know how much he meant to the Leeds and Juventus fans especially. He had been over in Italy and was taken ill while filming for a television show there. I was back in Wales when it happened and I didn't know much about the exact ins and outs of his illness at the time, but it soon became clear that John was in a bad way, and we were told to prepare for the worst. It's hard to describe the feeling of numbness that goes through you when you hear that someone so close to you is on the brink of dying. Dark thoughts just fly around your head and you don't know whether you're coming or going. I suppose you just hope that it's all a bad dream that you are going to wake up from and try to deny that it is really happening, but the reality of John's grave condition was something that the whole family and the country had to face up to with sadness and grief. They flew him back to Yorkshire, but couldn't save him and he died in a hospital in Wakefield a month after he had collapsed in Italy, passing away on 21 February 2004.

I went up to Leeds for the funeral, which was fittingly held on St David's Day, and the turnout was fantastic. Although it was such a sad time, it did warm my heart to see how many people's lives he had touched and what he had meant to them. All the tributes that poured in were so touching and each one left a lump in the throat. I idolised John as a kid, and he was always a big hero for me. He was a big hero to thousands more too and I was honoured to share my memories with them. Marcello Lippi, who was the Juventus coach at the time of his death, said: 'A really great person has left us. One thing about him that really left an impression on me was that whenever he spoke of Juventus, of its past or of its present, his eyes twinkled.' Big Jackie Charlton, my old pal from when I was on the ground staff at Leeds as a teenager and who had played alongside him at Elland Road, said of John: 'What a big strong man he was. They called him "the Gentle Giant". He was the best header of a ball I ever saw in my life.' And Sir Bobby Robson, one of the many who spoke in glowing terms of John – too many to mention – possibly summed him up best when he added: 'John wasn't only one of the greatest footballers who ever lived. He was one of the greatest men ever to have played the game.'

The public also paid their respects and tributes in their thousands – the fans were always important to John, as they were to me too. A memorial book for John was opened up in the Guildhall in Swansea and thousands of people left beautiful, heart-warming messages. A couple of months after his funeral in

Leeds, a memorial service was held in Brangwyn Hall in Swansea, and his widow Glenda bequeathed his ashes to the city. Wherever we had been in the world, our hearts always belonged to Swansea and it was a lovely gesture.

John's death hit me like a sledgehammer and I simply could not believe that he was gone. It was a desperately sad time for all the family, especially his four kids, but I feel he is still with us. Us Welsh are very emotional people; in fact I am the type that finds tears running down my cheeks when I'm just watching a film at home, but I think that's a quality we should be proud of. We are not scared to show our feelings and I think that helped me through those days after my brother's death. But like I say, I feel he is still with me and part of me. Even now, five years after he passed away, I still think he's up there and with me in spirit. I think all those years of being apart from him and thinking about him from afar have programmed me to believe that he's always going to be there, looking out for me, which always consoles and soothes me a lot. I think about him every day, without fail. I know that John is around somewhere, thinking of me.

They may have expected me to be a chip off the same block and at times it was a terrible burden, but while I may have lived in John's shadow as his younger brother, it was a wonderful shadow to be in.

CHAPTER 2
THE SHIRT OFF PELÉ'S BACK

'Nobody believed Wales could give us any trouble. Confidence is good, even necessary, but over-confidence can be a dangerous thing. Possibly because of this over-confidence we found ourselves in the toughest struggle of the tournament.'
PELÉ, MY LIFE AND THE BEAUTIFUL GAME

WHEN YOU'RE 23 YEARS OLD, with your whole career and life stretching out in front of you, it's hard to imagine that one game is going to represent the pinnacle of your career. There will be plenty more like this to come, you think. World Cups come along every four years. It's just another game, right? But as time has proved, and I look back on it 50 years down the line, Wales v Brazil in the quarter-finals of the 1958 World Cup was no ordinary game. Nor was Pelé ordinary. He was the player who broke our hearts in Gothenburg with the only goal of the game – and for all he went on to become the greatest footballer the world has ever seen, it was a rotten goal too, possibly the worst he ever scored!

With our shrewd and wily manager Jimmy Murphy pulling the strings, stirring the patriotic feelings within us and getting us playing to our strengths, a squad of unheralded but proud Welshmen had seized the chance to show the world what we could do in Sweden, putting the more-fancied English and Scots in the shade by reaching the quarter-finals. Northern Ireland were there too, the only time the four nations have made it together to the World Cup finals. We were punching above our weight and loving every minute of it. But by the time we got to our date with destiny against Pelé and Brazil in the Nya Ullevi Stadium in Gothenburg on 18 June 1958, we knew we would have to play to an almost superhuman level to get a result. Not only that, we had to do it without our best player, my brother John, who had been kicked off the park against Hungary in the previous game, a play-off match just 48 hours earlier. With no time left for our physios to work miracles, John didn't recover in time and reluctantly he had to sit and watch the match in his suit from the bench, roaring us on from the sidelines despite his frustration at not being able to play.

We didn't know much about Brazil as a team, but we knew they were good and that they were the red-hot favourites to win the World Cup. It was Pelé's very first World Cup match and only his second ever for his country, as he had been injured for the earlier matches. He was only 17, but there was a lot of hype about him going into the tournament and word quickly spread that Brazil had this incredibly gifted teenager ready to unleash his talent on the world. They had another amazing player called Garrincha, the Little Bird, who played outside right for them, and my team-mate Mel Hopkins couldn't believe it when he first saw him – looks were certainly deceptive in his case. I think Garrincha had contracted polio as a kid and because of that his feet were twisted at a strange angle, but boy could he could run like the wind – he was a flying machine! They had guys like Didi, Zagallo and Altifini in their team, and throw a couple of great attacking half-backs into the mix and you could see why they were such a marvellous side. They would just come piling forward at you, again and again, like a never-ending yellow wave. We found it hard to keep tabs on them because they would simply stream forward all the time. The sheer effort of having to maintain concentration was a draining experience. For all they were an attacking side though, I don't recall them being that dangerous in front of goal and to be honest we had the better chances to make the breakthrough. Colin Webster, the Manchester United striker who was standing in at centre-forward in the absence of John, shot wide in the first minute, then Cliffy Jones and Ivor Allchurch both hit the woodwork. It would have been interesting to have seen how they responded if little Wales had gone one-up, particularly as our game had been so strong defensively. Brazil did have a few half-chances, but they weren't the same team against us in the match that they later proved themselves to be in the semi-final and final. The reason for Brazil being a little subdued was that we never let them play the way that they liked. We played ultra defensive because Jimmy Murphy decided that was the best way to combat them, and by and large it worked.

But just as our game-plan seemed to be working a treat and Wales were threatening to pull off one of the biggest upsets of all time, Pelé went and stuck his oar in.

The goal still makes me shudder now. Pelé miskicked it, pure and simple. Garrincha put a ball into the box from the right and Pelé got in just in front of me to take the ball on his chest, swivel, then squeeze a shot in from just outside the six-yard box. I say a shot, but it was more like a pass-back, with a little help from his shin. It rolled in like a golf putt, and not a very good one at that. It wasn't one of the great shots that he became famed for over the years – he seemed to kick the ground first and the ball ricocheted up off Stuart Williams' foot and started trickling towards the net. Our keeper Jack Kelsey must have seen the ball heading towards the net in slow motion, but he just couldn't get across to it. It was probably the worst goal Pelé ever scored! I was downhearted after that and took a lot of picking up. I can still see the goal clear as crystal now, and it upsets me to this day. The reaction to the goal within the stadium was incredible; it seemed like time had stood still and maybe that's why I have such a clear vision of it now. While I gaped open-mouthed at the ball in the back of the net, an elated Pelé went rushing in after it, slid to his knees and lifted the ball above his head like it was the Jules Rimet trophy itself. He had good reason to, I suppose – maybe he already sensed how special that goal would be to him, his first of many in the World Cup. The boy who would be king had just become the youngest player ever to score a goal at the World Cup finals, aged 17 years and 239 days. Three or four of his team-mates slid into the goal after him and they formed a huddle at the back of the net. To add to the pandemonium, half-a-dozen photographers dashed onto the pitch to capture the moment, almost barging us out the way like we had no right being there in order to aim their cameras at the celebrating Brazilians, and Pelé in particular. We just wanted to get the ball back off him and get on with the game. We might have gone 1-0 down to the best team in the world, but we had come that far and we weren't ready to give up just then. I felt like shouting at them all to clear off and give me the ball, but my throat had gone dry and I was, for once, lost for words.

There was a cracking documentary that they showed recently on the Welsh language television station S4C, marking the 50th anniversary of the game, and it was interesting to hear Pelé's thoughts on the match all those years later. Give him his due, he gave a lot of credit to Wales, and he admitted that Brazil were in one hell of a game that night in Gothenburg. I didn't really stick in when we were doing Welsh at school, apart from the times I was cheating and copying from the boy next to me, but Pelé was quoted as saying: 'It was a difficult game but I have good memories as I scored the goal that took Brazil to the semi-finals and, eventually, led us to win the World Cup. That goal gave me confidence. Wales marked very tightly at the back and I remember getting the ball, turning and squeezing it into the corner of the net. I consider it the most important goal I've ever scored – it gave me the confidence to continue my career.

'I knew Wales could defend well and were good on the counter-attack. It was a relief for us, but a tragedy for the game that John Charles had been injured and could not play. Being able to play was a great experience. I was a little nervous but I didn't carry the huge pressure to perform that rested on the shoulders of experienced players like Didi, Nilton Santos, Zito and Vavá and the brilliant goalkeeper, Gilmar.'

That was Pelé speaking 50 years after the game, but the teenage Pelé also said some nice things about me immediately after that World Cup too, particularly that I was the best centre-half at the tournament, which still means a lot to me to this day. Coming from such a great player it fills me with pride. It was nice to be officially recognised too when FIFA named me in the best eleven in the World Cup – obviously Pelé's words carried a bit of weight even when he was a teenager! I just seemed to hit form at the right time at the World Cup and it helps of course when you have games coming at you thick and fast. As soon as one match finishes, the adrenaline is still pumping and you just want to get on with the next game. It's a good feeling when you're playing well, and it puts an added spring in your step and ensures that you lose any fear or nerves. That's the secret to any team doing well at a World Cup, I think, just getting a bit of momentum and confidence behind them.

You couldn't have said anything to me straight after the match, though. I was more or less inconsolable. We were all a bit upset in the dressing room, coming to terms with the realisation that our chance was gone and our World Cup was over, just as we were starting to really enjoy ourselves. But we did our best and we did very well too. We could hold our heads up high and be proud of what we had done for ourselves as individuals and as a team, and for Wales as a country, and when Brazil went on to win the tournament, with Pelé as the star of the show, it just showed you how well we had done to come so close to beating them.

Our manager Jimmy Murphy wasn't really one for showing his emotions, but even he was welling up a bit after the game. He told reporters as they scrambled for a few words with him afterwards: 'I am the last fellow in the world to make excuses but with John Charles in the side we might have won.' To be honest, he was spot-on. John would have made the difference in that game. Brazil were a small team in terms of height and I think they would have really struggled to handle the aerial threat John would have carried. No offence to his stand-in for the game, Colin Webster, who was a great player in his own right, but he was only little and he didn't carry the same threat. I think we definitely could have beaten them with John in the side. Brazil would have spent a lot of the time worrying about the threat that he carried, and that might just have allowed us to exploit them. The truth is, in what was a mighty close match anyway, we had been forced to play without our best player and I reckon John would have swung it our way.

John had still been great to have in the dressing room before the game, and he did all he could to motivate us, doing his best to hide his own anguish at having to sit it out. He told us not to worry, that he would be fit for the semi-final, and he gave us a lot of belief that we could go out and match Brazil and had nothing to fear. But in later years he would confess that missing that one game was his biggest disappointment in football, and he said in an interview after he had finished playing: 'If it had been 24 hours later I would have dragged myself onto the pitch. What always makes things worse was that I honestly believed we would make the World Cup final that year. If we could have got into the last two, who knows what might have happened? Why couldn't we have been the world kings?'

The truth was that we did match Brazil, and before Pelé's crucial intervention it could have been Wales who nicked the goal, not them. We defended like our lives depended on it, and although I still play the goal over and over in my head to see if I could have done more to stop Pelé scoring, I was proud of the way me and my team-mates played. Immediately after the game, Jimmy Murphy had nothing but glowing praise for our defensive efforts against Brazil. 'We have the best defence in the four home countries,' he declared – and he was right, we had outshone England, Scotland and Northern Ireland at the finals and though our tactics had been defensive at times, we did what we had to do.

After the Brazil game we stayed in Sweden one more day and then came back. We flew back to London before getting the train back home to Swansea and cold reality – and talk about coming back down to earth with a bump. To give you an idea of how badly publicised the World Cup was 50 years ago, when I got back to the station in Swansea with Terry Medwin and Cliffy Jones, the ticket collector casually came up to us and said to me 'Where have you been, Mel – away on your holidays again?' I looked at him with astonishment, first thinking he was just pulling my leg but then realising that he really didn't have the foggiest where we had been. I could only spit out a reply: 'I was at the World Cup, you prat!' That's how well known we were! I don't think a lot of people in Wales even knew the World Cup was on.

We did well for ourselves and the country. We weren't appreciated when we came back home, but only because people didn't realise what we had done, they didn't know what we had achieved. It's only now, when we've celebrated the 50th anniversary of what we did in Sweden with interviews, documentaries and presentations, that people appreciate just how well Wales did as a nation at the World Cup in 1958 – a far cry from the way it had been at the time. Today there would be open-top buses and a big parade – we would have been treated like heroes, but there was nothing like that then. Christ, I think they might even have been talking about knighthoods for us all. Sir John, Sir Mel, Sir Cliff, Sir Jack… no, perhaps not!

In fact, the *South Wales Evening Post* didn't even have us as the main story on their back page the day after the Brazil game – it was a bloody Glamorgan cricket match against Essex that stole all the headlines! Can you believe it? Good God, county cricket first in the batting order instead of a World Cup game, and not just any World Cup game – it was the quarter-finals! Virtually no one had a television in those days and if that was the attitude the newspaper editors were taking, then it's little wonder some people didn't even know where we were.

But the match report, tucked away on a little side column, was something of a hidden gem and was packed full of kind words for our efforts. The newspaper's reporter Bill McGowran, who had been out in Sweden with us, wrote in his article from Gothenburg: 'Wales fought gloriously to the last ditch of their World Cup quarter-final with Brazil. The South Americans, favourites to win the title, only scored one goal – and that a lucky one – against a weakened Welsh side, dog-tired and leg-weary after five strenuous matches in a week. There was no need to make alibis or excuses for this magnificent bunch of big-hearted battlers.'

And the journalist also had incredibly generous words for me and my fellow Wales defenders, echoing the words of Jimmy. 'The collective transfer value of Kelsey, Hopkins, Williams and Mel Charles would almost pay off the national debt,' he wrote. 'I heard two Brazilians arguing: "Our forwards can't get going tonight," said the first, to which the other replied, "Who could get going against such a defence as this?" All of the Welsh rearguard deserve medals of purest platinum, but the greatest of them all in this Homeric match was Mel Charles, who upheld the family honour by doing two men's work as if burning to compensate for the absence of brother John.'

Nice words and they still make me blush now! Perhaps I should have hired him as my agent, because it all helped to build up my reputation and it was only a matter of time before Swansea Town – already well known for being something of a selling club – decided they had an asset on their hands that they could cash in on.

It may have been a low-key journey back to Wales, but among the souvenirs in my suitcase was Pelé's shirt, which really should have been the most treasured memento for any player to take back, except I didn't have the faintest idea exactly what it would come to symbolise. At the end of the game, Pelé had just come over and shaken hands with me and I got his shirt, blissfully unaware that the fresh-faced teenager would go on to become one of the biggest superstars, if not THE biggest, the world of football has ever seen. He may have scored the goal that knocked us out the World Cup but at least I had the shirt off Pelé's back!

Whereas nowadays you hear of players insuring shirts they have swapped with star players during their careers and locking them in air-tight vaults, with alarms and insurance policies, I didn't have the foresight to bother with any of that malarkey. The famous shirt led something of a colourful life from the moment I brought it back to Wales. When I finished playing football I ran a Sunday league pub team in Swansea – The Travellers, they were called – and we didn't have any money to buy shirts, so I brought down all my international shirts that I had collected over the years for the boys to pull on. I wanted them to at least feel like footballers, and the way I saw it the shirts were just lying about the house gathering dust, so I might as well put them to good use. If I hadn't come up with the shirts they wouldn't have been able to play, as there was no money available to be splashing out on kit. I suppose I should have had those strips locked away and kept safe for the future, but I didn't really place any special sentimental value on them. So when I went down to the park to dish out the strips to all the lads I had the greens of Ireland, blues of Scotland, whites of England, reds of Wales – anything I could lay my hands on, really. We had a lad called Brian O'Shea, who was Irish, so he naturally made a beeline to get the Irish shirt, and there was a Scotsman who pounced on the blue one. What a sight we must have looked – the league of nations! And at the end of the game, when they were splattered in mud, they were all just unceremoniously bundled into a bag and slung into the washing machine together. I think Pelé's poor shirt ended up about seven different colours by the time it had gone through the wash a few times! I've still got it – well, my son Jeremy has it – but its colour has changed badly for the worse and it's probably worth next to nothing, other than the sentimental value I have finally recognised that it holds. I think Pelé would see the funny side of it though, and would probably even approve of the fact that a pub team player had got to run about in his shirt. After all, the beautiful game is for all footballers, from the World Cup to the public parks of Swansea.

CHAPTER 3
ALICE STREET WONDERLAND

'John and Melvyn have been soccer crazy ever since I can remember. At home their mother seldom saw them. They spent every moment of their spare time in the fields and parks around Swansea kicking a ball about.'
NED CHARLES, 1958

IF IT HADN'T BEEN FOR A STURDY, corrugated roof, protected by a layer of turf and earth, you would never have heard of John Charles. Or Mel Charles for that matter! As the sirens blared out in the middle of the night, the two of us had scurried as fast as our little legs would carry us into the Anderson shelter at the bottom of the garden along with the rest of the Charles family. The Luftwaffe were bombing the hell out of my hometown, Swansea, as the Second World War raged on, and when the sirens sounded you ran like hell and got yourself as safe as you could possibly could. With all of us huddled inside, listening to the explosions as they got closer and closer, the shelter took a direct hit when an incendiary bomb thumped right into the roof. Mercifully we all lived to tell the tale.

There is now a plaque on the wall outside our old terraced house at Number 9 Alice Street that reads 'Wonderland'. For us, that's a perfect description of the home we grew up in – and it was in this house where it all started for me and John.

Melvyn Charles arrived screaming and kicking into the world on the 14 May 1935, a second son for my father Edward, or Ned as everybody knew him, and my mother Lilian. My name is actually spelt the Welsh way on my birth certificate, with an F, but I was always happy enough being Melvyn rather than Melfyn. My sister Maureen had come first, then John, who was born on the 27 December 1931. Our little brother Malcolm and sister Avril completed the family.

Although we didn't have two ha'pennys to rub together growing up, I've got nothing but happy memories from my childhood – apart from the odd brotherly fight with John, of course, and the odd clip round the ear from my father. But boys will be boys.

There were no airs and graces in our house; there couldn't be when there were two families living under the same roof, all living on top of one another with privacy a non-starter. My mother's sister, my Auntie Theresa, lived in the kitchen, and we lived in the middle room. When the people at number six, a couple of doors along, moved on somewhere else, the whole lot of us moved into that house. I think we just bundled everything into boxes and carried them down the street, it wasn't much of a flit. We always felt happy and content in Alice Street and we were surrounded by a lot of good neighbours. The sense of community was strong in Cwmbwrla and despite the lack of money, everyone got on well.

My father had been in the Navy during the First World War and was torpedoed twice in the North Sea. He settled back in Swansea at the end of his military service and was a hard grafter as a steel erector in the steelworks at Margam, on the outskirts of the city. My mother worked just as hard, in her own way. As a housewife and cleaner she was the one who kept the house ticking over and she did a damn good job of it, not that a couple of lads with their heads full of football and a few other capers paid too much attention. My mother didn't know anything about football, but she worked her fingers to the bone every day cleaning other houses and seeing to it that we were happy. She was just as determined as my dad to make sure there was food on the table and provide us with what little clothes we could afford. It's incredible how we survived in those days, but somehow we did. She didn't really get football though; it was something completely alien to her. When we were older, she was watching us play for Wales in a game against England and she leapt to her feet in the stand shouting at the top of her voice: 'My boy has scored! My boy has scored!' The only problem was that John had been defending a corner at the time and had just headed the ball into his own net! There must have been a few looks of embarrassment on the spectators around her, but although she didn't understand what was going on, I do know that she was proud to see her boys represent Wales.

John and I weren't really the types to be hanging around the house – we were quite happy to go and cause trouble somewhere else. The two of us made our own entertainment, and used to play hopscotch, whip and top, and of course football, following in the footsteps of the old man, who had been a decent player himself. As a youngster he played for the Sunday school side at St Luke's Church in Cwmbwrla and they won the league and cup double.

As an adult, he played at left half-back with Swansea Town amateurs before he broke his leg in a game at Cwmbwrla Park, when he was playing for Cwm Mission. He'd won a few cups and medals himself as an amateur and for a while he was invited to play in mid Wales for Llandrindod Wells, where he used to get paid in pints of beer – which suited him nicely, ta very much! He even played in a cup final down at the Vetch and they went to the game in a horse and cart because there were no buses in those days.

While he had been a keen player himself, our father didn't really take too much interest in our football to begin with because he was such a hard grafter and liked a drink after work. But, while he wasn't the pushy type, there's no doubt that we still picked up the football habit from our dad. It was in our genes, I suppose. We didn't own a ball, but every day in the summer holidays we would bail out of the house at nine o'clock in the morning and not return home until eight in the evening, sometimes later, whenever it was starting to get dark. We didn't even worry about getting food down our necks – our stomachs came a poor second when there was football to be played. Almost as soon as we were awake, we just got our shoes on and headed to 'our' park, Cwmbwrla Park, which was just a couple of hundred yards away from the house. At the time, it was known locally as Williams Farm as well, but everyone now knows it as Cwmbwrla Park. We had a fight on our hands a few years back to stop houses being built on the park, but it is now protected by law after the council stepped in, and thankfully it will stay as playing fields forever. It would have been a tragedy had the developers, in the name of making a fast buck, been allowed to wipe away what has been such an important facility for the community, and a place that has become symbolic for its part in Welsh football history. A lot of internationals were produced from the rag-tag bunch of boys that used to while away the hours in Cwmbwrla Park — Mel Nurse, Ivor Allchurch, Lenny Allchurch, John, myself, my cousins, Jackie Roberts, Ernie Jones, plus Glyn Davies who went on to play for Derby, to name just a few. We all came from that one little area of Swansea, which became a hotbed for promising young footballers, and even drew scouts along as they tried to tap into a steady conveyor belt of talent. If there were a hundred kids kicking a ball about in a park, a professional club would be happy to settle for one out of that hundred making it as a player, but Cwmbwrla was an exception to the rule. The percentage of special players was way above the average. We were all able to learn from each other, whether it was how to control a ball, how to kick with both feet, or just how to look after yourself physically when there's a few dozen eager young lads chasing after one ball. It brought everyone's game on, but it brought on the special ones even more. It's fantastic to think how many players came out of there, something all of us should be proud of. Perhaps there was something in the water.

A couple of jackets would be thrown down in the park and we'd play in games that could grow into thirty-a-side epics. Players arriving late would simply be added to each team as they turned up one by one, and the games were always fiercely competitive. It gave a lot of us a will to win and do well at an early age. Nobody wanted to be in the losing side and if you didn't win sometimes you would go off to bed in a real mood, waiting to get sleep out the way so you could redress the balance in the game the next day. Sometimes it would be Alice Street against a team we called The Backs and we wouldn't leave the park until we had run ourselves into the ground or it was nearing pitch black.

None of us could afford proper football boots, but once I had a pair of boots I was quite proud of. My dad fancied himself as a bit of a cobbler and he had pulled off a really neat trick by adding leather strips to the sides of my shoes, which stopped me from slipping and sliding all over the pitch, which if it rained could become a bit of a mudbath. Once I'd got home from football, the strips would come off and the boots would become just normal boots again – John and I would be able to wear the boots to school as well. But when I put them down for goalposts one day some cheeky beggar nabbed them. I had hell to pay with my father for that, as you can imagine he was not best pleased.

My dad was proud of us most of the time though. He gave an interview to the *Empire News* in 1958 and told them: 'John and Melvyn have been soccer-crazy ever since I can remember. At home their mother seldom saw them. They spent every moment of their spare time in the fields and parks around Swansea kicking a ball about.'

After the incident in the Anderson shelter when the bomb had slammed into the roof, we swapped the city for a bit of country life. The war broke us up as a family for a while. Swansea was being bombed to bits and it wasn't a safe place for kids, so it wasn't long before we were told that we were to be sent out of harm's way to the countryside for a while. We were eventually evacuated to Llandeilo in Carmarthenshire, west of Swansea and safe from the war planes. It was 1941 and I was only six years old. Me and my big sister, Maureen, were sent to one house, staying on a farm, and John stayed with another family about two miles down the road, also on a farm – all a far cry from Swansea. It was the first time I'd been on a train in my life and I still remember standing there on the platform, wide-eyed and a little bit scared, clutching my gas mask as if my life depended on it.

We stayed in Llandeilo for about three or four months, but while Maureen looked after me and kept things nice and calm, John was busy raising hell at the other house – he got sent home before us because he had killed so many chickens! He and another lad, Danny Sullivan, had been killing them because I think they were hoping to sell them to raise some extra pennies.

Any news that filtered through about John I just got on the local grapevine, as there wasn't really any opportunity to meet up or stay in touch during the evacuation. The people in Llandeilo were very nice and welcomed us in to their community, and while I missed all the adventures of Alice Street, it was a good experience and a pleasant change from the norm even at that age. When you're a kid everything is an adventure and it never even crossed my mind that my parents might still be in some kind of danger back in Swansea. We went to a primary school called Golden Grove and were taught how to speak a little bit of Welsh there; we used to hop onto the back of an old post-office cart when it stopped at the farm and get a lift. I have been back to see the old school building since and it's still there after all that time. It's amazing and brings back a lot of happy memories.

When it was decided that it was all clear and more or less safe to head for Swansea again, John and I were together again, and we didn't waste any time getting back into our football and getting into scrapes. I was like his shadow at times. It's only natural that you look up to your big brother and I wasn't any different – to me he was the governor. There were nearly four years between us, but we got along just fine and although there were times when we fought like hell, he was always there to look out for me if I was in any trouble myself.

I got all John's clothes handed down to me, and whether they fitted or not, it made no difference. I had to go to the senior school in short trousers, when I wanted to have longs on. Generally I enjoyed my schooldays though, if not the actual lessons. John first went to school in Cwmbwrla and I soon followed, and I again had the teachers groaning when I followed him through the doors of Manselton Senior School – well, all the teachers except the ones that took us for football. We weren't exactly known for sticking in at lessons, and we were hauled up in front of the teacher for the cane once or twice. But when it came to sports it was a different matter altogether, and you could count on the Charles brothers to give football, cricket, boxing and any other sport going their full, undivided attention. When I went on to senior school at Manselton I was dead keen on just about any sport available, but I played mainly cricket and football there. We had a memorable game of cricket just before Christmas, the challenge being that the lad who hit the most runs would get ten shillings. Ten shillings was a lot of money then. I won it by hitting a hundred-odd runs and remember being well chuffed with myself. You could buy a pair of shoes with ten shillings then, although I don't think I spent the cash on anything quite so practical, and I seem to remember having a lot of new 'friends' the moment the money was handed over to me.

The staff at Manselton were pretty proud of their football team especially, and their teams generally had a good track record, not just locally but in producing players for the Swansea Schoolboys select side as well.

But while we might have excelled on the sports field I wasn't at all academic. I liked maths and that was probably my best subject. Anyone who knows me will laugh at this, but I came top in Welsh as well, although I have to confess I barely know a word of the language. But back then I found an easy way to go straight to the top of the class, without having to tax my brain too much.

It helped that the boy at the next desk was Welsh-speaking and a bit of a brainbox too, and it helped even more that I had a good view of his desk. I just started taking a crafty peek whenever he wasn't looking and more importantly, whenever the teacher wasn't paying attention, and copied down what he was writing. It worked a treat and they sent me to the top of the class with top marks, 20 out of 20! The same boy was shocked to find himself with an unexpected rival for top marks, and curiosity got the better of him when he couldn't help but come over to ask me: 'Hey Mel, I didn't know you spoke Welsh?' To my shame, I just tried to lie my way through it by telling him that my mother spoke Welsh! I never did get rumbled for that one – until now, that is! I think I may be a bit old for the cane, though.

The teachers at school were generally okay towards me. I did get the cane from time to time though; I think you were viewed as a bit of a softy by the other kids if you didn't. My main problem and the reason for most of my clashes with the teachers was that I was always late for school. First thing in the morning we would get together in the hall and the headmaster would make you stand either left or right of him, depending on whether you had arrived at the school gates late or not, so he could take the register. If you were late you had to stand up on the left-hand side, and when he worked his way down the list and came to 'Mel Charles', he would automatically look to the left without fail because he knew nine times out of ten that was where I would be standing! I used to just get distracted on the way in, dawdling along without a care in the world, and for that reason I was always late and in danger of risking a few smacks of the cane.

I didn't really pay attention during lessons either and that was to cause me a few problems later in life, because I hadn't grasped the basics of reading and writing at all when I left school. Sport was the only thing I was really interested in; maybe because it was something I was naturally able to do well in. Football was our life, even then. If you were in the school team you found that you got a bit spoilt by the teachers; they would cut you some slack and keep you sweet because they always wanted the school team to do well. I was never a model pupil though. You had to go to school just because it was somewhere to go, although sometimes they would come looking for me if I'd been playing truant – I'd be hiding round the back of the house somewhere whenever the truant officer came knocking at the door. But I would always make sure I was in school on a Friday, because that's when we had football. When I was at Manselton it overlooks a big hill, 'the racecourse' we called it, and we thought we'd go looking for birds' eggs to collect, and the teacher spotted us from the school building with a set of binoculars. I got the cane for that particular adventure as well.

A lot of people reckoned John and I would have made perfect rugby players because of our physique, but the truth is that we didn't have rugby on the curriculum at the two schools we attended. I'm sure that surprises many folk, with Wales boasting such a great rugby tradition, but it was never an option for us, and even if it had been I don't think there is any way we would have been prepared to give up football for it. While football was our true love, we were also good cricketers and boxers, and John even toyed with the idea of taking it up seriously in the ring after being urged to do so by a teacher, Herbie Morris, who had been impressed with him at the boxing club we had at Manselton. We both seemed to have a natural knack for sports, although we weren't very big in these days, and I especially was a real titch. I know people must have looked at us during our days as footballers and thought that we had always been big, strapping lads, but neither of us really sprouted until well into our teens. Our father wasn't that tall, so for us both to go past the six-foot barrier was a bit of surprise. Despite the lure of boxing and other sports, I am one hundred per cent confident we made the right choice by deciding to make football our number one sport. I was influenced a lot by what John did in those days – like I said, I was his shadow. When he boxed, I boxed. When he got a paper round, I got a paper round. When he joined the army cadets... yes, you've guessed it, I joined the army cadets too. To be honest, we only joined the cadets so we could get our hands on the uniform they dished out for free. We were sick of going to school in short trousers and the army cadets handed out long trousers as well as a brown shirt and boots, so that alone was enough of an incentive to join up. It made you feel grown-up all of a sudden, wearing those long trousers.

John always looked after me as a kid. If I got into fights he would step in for me and protect his little brother, but that's not to say that we didn't have our share of battles – it's all part of growing up, isn't it? Having your big brother knocking seven bells out of you! I remember one time we had a big fight over fireworks. I was always easily swayed by John because I looked up to him so much and wanted to keep him happy. But he knew that too, and he was cunning enough to know that he could use it to his advantage at times. When it was getting close to Guy Fawkes Night, he kept me off school for a week just so I could go round the streets with him collecting a penny for the guy. He obviously thought that having his little brother in tow would help people dip into their pockets and add a few more pennies or sweets to the stash. We did okay, and he was off with the money that he had collected buying bangers and rockets, but when it came to the big night on Guy Fawkes all he would give me were the sparklers – I felt exploited, he'd stitched me right up! There was another time we fought over some pet rabbits that we had. John had a little black one and I had a white one and when his died, John wanted my rabbit – cue another big fight.

We fought like hell at times, even though he was bigger than me, but we were contented kids. They were really happy times and despite the fact there was hardly ever any money around to keep us in clothes and food, we never thought anything of it. We had been given a strong family upbringing and had some good values passed on to us. The fights with John also helped toughen me up, although they didn't happen too often and most of the time we got along just fine. I was a real titch as a kid, while John was already starting to fill out a bit and although he didn't really start growing to his full height until he was about 16, already he was on the way to becoming the Gentle Giant.

CHAPTER 4
ESCAPE FROM ELLAND ROAD

'My reason for leaving Leeds was homesickness, pure and simple. It was gnawing away at me and you think to yourself what kind of life is this?'
MEL CHARLES

WHEN JOHN SIGNED FOR LEEDS there was a bit of a kerfuffle because Swansea thought he was all set to sign for them. His talent was already pretty well known in Swansea, he'd been a star in the schoolboy ranks, and the club were happy to give him his first taste of life at a professional football club at the age of 14. The only problem was that Swansea went about it all the wrong way and ended up paying the price for not being a bit more careful, something they were to forever regret. John was on the ground staff getting fifteen shillings a week after being spotted by the club's scout and trainer Joe Sykes, a former player with Swansea. John had been playing in matches in the Welsh League, but because he had only been registered on amateur forms there was nothing Swansea could do to stop him leaving anytime he wanted and signing for someone else. It was a loophole waiting to be exploited and as it turned out it was Leeds who were the ones to benefit.

Trevor Ford and Roy Paul were, in common with most starry-eyed Swansea boys, John's big heroes at the time he was on the ground staff. He used to really look up to them and Roy was something of a role model for him, so much so that John hung on to his every word, picking up all the little snippets of information and football knowledge that helped shape him into such a complete player in later years. John followed Roy Paul around so much that apparently he joked to the other players that the eager apprentice should be called his 'Shadow' – but I think Roy was probably flattered at the same time that someone much younger was willing to listen, watch and learn, and he had also spotted the potential in John even at that tender age. Roy Paul was one of the players that inspired schoolboys like ourselves to dream of being footballers. He left the Swans under a bit of a cloud. He went to Bogota and signed for a Colombian side, only to come back within weeks when it never worked out. But the damage was done between him and the Swans' board and they soon flogged him to Manchester City. At a time when transfer fees started to creep up year after year, Trevor Ford became the most expensive forward in Britain when Swansea sold him to Sunderland for £30,000 in 1950. He was quite a player too and for years had the honour of being the top scorer for Wales along with Ivor Allchurch, until a certain goal machine called Ian Rush came along and broke their record.

Joe Sykes, who was to go on to become a big influence on my career at the Vetch, had been singing the praises of John and tipping him for great things in the future, but for all Joe was bubbling over with enthusiasm about the kid he thought had the lot, the man who mattered most – the manager – still needed to be convinced and the truth was that he was in no hurry to start rushing him towards the fringes of the first team at a critical time for the Swans. Billy McCandless, who had taken over from Haydn Jones as the boss at the Vetch, was content to bide his time with the youngsters and try to nurse them along a little bit first before throwing them in, and you probably couldn't fault this cautious way of thinking. It was a time when the Swans desperately needed results and battle-hardened pros to get them back on the up and up after they had been relegated to the Third Division in 1947. On the face of it, the cut-throat environment of the Third Division definitely wasn't the right place to be experimenting with precocious teenagers who still had a lot to prove. When you're down in the Third Division the books need to be balanced and people's livelihoods are on the line if you can't get out of there fast – well, that certainly applied to Swansea, who were far too big a club to be languishing away down in that league. There was no Fourth Division then, just a Third Division split into two, north and south, and as you can probably imagine it was no glamour league. It was a tough place to be playing football, with a lot of clubs and players down on their luck. I can see now why McCandless was so reluctant to pitch young apprentices into such a hard and unforgiving league, no matter how good and promising they were. He wouldn't have lasted long in his job had he sent out a team of kids on a whim and found they were treading water.

But for all that, the nagging, gnawing feeling among those closest to him was that John wasn't getting a fair chance with the Swans. He was a footballer waiting to happen, but he wasn't really one for waiting too long at anything. Like me, he just couldn't keep still most of the time, he had to be on the move, and needed things to be happening for him quickly or frustration would set in. Being stuck on the ground-staff doing odd jobs must have been driving him barmy. He would turn out for a local team, Gendros, to keep himself ticking over football-wise, and was also known to still kick a ball about with his little brother and the rest of the boys down at Cwmbwrla Park. As fate would have it, it was during one of these park kickabouts that he was spotted by the Leeds scout who operated in our neck of the woods, a bloke called Jack Pickard. He was mesmerised as he watched John running rings round everyone, not including me of course, but when Pickard made some gentle enquiries he just assumed that because John was already on the ground staff with the Swans, he would have to keep his distance and look elsewhere.

But then my dad intervened. He wasn't happy that John hadn't yet been given his chance with Swansea and he felt that he was being paid a pittance for what amounted to a series of menial jobs, like sweeping the North Bank at the Vetch, weeding the track round the pitch, and painting the grandstand. Jobs like these were part of the role of any apprentice then, but they only did it in the hope that their chance wouldn't be too far round the corner, and for John it didn't seem that that chance was going to happen anytime soon.

My father thought John was overdue his chance, and besides that he also thought it was time he was bringing more money into the house, because by then the big fellow was eating like a horse and growing out of his clothes at a rate of knots. More hand-me-downs were piled up for me to wear as he went through trousers and shoes like nobody's business. As soon as he grew out of them, then I would be jumping into them – I was a growing lad too. Dad knew Jack Pickard had sent players up to

Leeds for a trial before and explained that because John, who by then was 16, was only on amateur forms with the Swans, there was nothing stopping the scout from at least taking him up to Elland Road for a trial.

Leeds were operating within the rules of that time and were doing nothing wrong, but I know that people in Swansea saw it differently from a moral point of view, and felt that Leeds were stealing one of their own. I was actually in the house on the day that Pickard came to our door to invite John up north, and I was sent to go and get him from the park where he was playing cricket at the time with some of his pals. Unwittingly, I had played a part, albeit a very small one, in snatching John away from the Swans. For that, I suppose I'd better say sorry to the people of Swansea!

There was a hell of an argument over the move, and a lot of bad feeling and resentment lingered around for years afterwards, some of it directed towards Jack Pickard, unfairly I reckon, but the transfer went through and John was the property of Leeds. Our mother didn't even know where the place was, which seems hilarious now. Welsh people didn't really move around much in those days and she was completely convinced that John would need to apply for a passport to get himself there, even though Leeds was just a couple of hundred miles away!

In 1950, and round about the same time that all that was going on, I had the honour of playing in the Swansea Schoolboys side that won the FA schools shield, the second time the town had brought the trophy home since the War, although the side that John had played in had only made it to the quarter-finals. Cliffy Jones, who would go on to become a great mate of mine with Swansea and with Wales, was the captain in our team, and in the final we travelled up to Manchester to beat their schoolboys in their own back yard. It was 1-0 in the final at Maine Road, a fantastic result. I remember there being a big crowd there and even though I knew what the atmosphere could be like at the Vetch when it was busy, it was another thing being out there on the pitch as a player and seeing it with your own eyes – thousands of people watching and reacting to your every move. While some schoolboys would get nervous playing in front of a big crowd, I was the opposite. I just thought to myself 'this will do me' and I think I definitely got a taste for it there and then. Although I was just gliding my way through life and still had no real idea what I wanted to do with myself when I left school, maybe that was the exact moment that I started to dream seriously of a career as a professional footballer, assuming I was going to be good enough.

With John starting a new life for himself at Leeds, where the great Major Frank Buckley was the governor at the time, I left school at 14 and was already playing for the local team, Stepney – a boy in a man's league. Pickard, who had already been getting a lot of stick around the town for taking John up to Leeds, came along and asked me if I wanted to go to Elland Road as well. It was a big risk though. Maybe it didn't seem so at the time, because I thought if John could do it, what was to stop me doing it as well? But I was young and naïve, and I didn't realise just how much of a fish out of water I would be, leaving my comfort zone in Swansea for a strange and lonely city. After what I went through up in Leeds, I wouldn't advise any kid to leave their home town if they had the chance of staying put, unless they are absolutely sure of what is waiting for them. That was the advice I would later put to good use when my boy Jeremy was weighing up offers from clubs all over the country. I told him not to make the same mistake that I had, and thankfully he listened to me and enjoyed some great times with the Swans.

But back then I thought I didn't have anything to lose and

everything to gain, and so I threw caution to the wind and went to Leeds, hoping that it would all work out and having no reason to think that it wouldn't. I got on well with the other young lads on the ground staff, even though they were all strangers to me at first. My big mate up there was Jackie Charlton, who used to stay in digs next door to me. We became close pals and I even used to go up to his home at weekends in Ashington, Northumberland, to meet his folks. I would see Bobby too of course, who was just a nipper, but even then he would be in a lane at the back of the house kicking a ball against the wall and laying the foundations for what was one of the greatest careers ever seen in English football. We used to call big Jackie Charlton 'fish', not so much because he'd developed a passion for fishing, but more because he had a big long neck like a fish! I've managed to catch up with Jackie a few times over the years, and he's been down in Wales a few times to do the after-dinner speaking, which he's absolutely fantastic at, but Bobby's a different type of bloke and I never really had too much to do with him.

Trips like the ones to Jackie's cheered me up, but I was down in the dumps most of the time I was at Leeds because I missed Swansea and all my mates there so much. When you're on your own in a strange city it can be tough. John wasn't even there at the time to help me through because he was away in the Army doing his National Service, something I would later do myself – again following in my big brother's footsteps.

Because I was on the ground staff I had to do things like cleaning the stands and the big banks of terraces, and they also had me scraping the weeds from the pitch. The first team players at Elland Road were absolutely marvellous towards me, however, and so was the Leeds manager, Major Frank Buckley. He had done wonders for John, taken him under his wing and started to mould his game and his life, and I think he looked out for me too because I was John's brother. Whether he spotted the same qualities in me as he did in John I don't know, but he always took an extra interest in how I was doing and was generally a smashing, if rather an intimidating guy. Because he had come from an army background you always had to call Major Buckley 'Sir', and whenever you saw him he would have his faithful dog by his side. The dog was called 'Bryn' after Bryn Jones, a player who had been at Leeds before my time and who had been a Wales international. I think Bryn must have been the Major's favourite player too, if he was willing to call his dog after him. Major Frank Buckley had been a good player himself and had managed a few clubs including Blackpool, Wolves and Hull before he became a legend at Leeds. But it was during the War where he had been a real hero and after fighting and being wounded in the Battle of the Somme that he rose to the rank of Major, the title by which everybody knew him, even when he was managing football teams. He may have been a fierce disciplinarian, but the influence he had on a lot of players' careers, including mine and John's, was massive. That's not to say he didn't scare the life out of you sometimes. He used to come down and everyone was frightened to death because he had a real air of authority about him. If you were of a nervous disposition and saw him coming, then you buggered off out of his way pronto, especially if you were slacking or up to no good. But fair play to him, most of the time he would say 'how are you doing, son? Stick in there and keep up the good work.'

Eventually, I graduated from the more menial tasks and I got to go inside and clean the first team players' boots, getting to know some of them a bit in the process. You had guys like Frank Dudley and Len Browning, who would look out for me and keep an eye on how I was doing and make me feel part of the club, even though I was just a kid. I was up at Leeds for around a year and never got home for any holidays because it was too expensive to travel all the way down to Wales. I used to stay in digs with a Mrs Webster. They were lovely people and looked after you, but the problem was you were on your own most of the time and all the solitude would drive you round the bend. You would just have to stay in because you were only 15 and a long way from home and your mates – there was nowhere for young people to go, especially if you never really knew your way round the town. Staying in wasn't the greatest of options either – there was no television in those days and I couldn't read. At times you could be sitting in your room bored out of your head, hoping something more interesting might come along like watching paint dry or counting the number of flowers on the wallpaper.

My reason for leaving Leeds was homesickness, pure and simple. It was gnawing away inside of me and eventually you reach the point where you think to yourself 'What kind of life is this?' When you're only a youngster and you can't do anything it starts to get on top of you. There was nowhere to socialise, well not anywhere I knew of as a lad from out of town – and I couldn't go drinking, I was far too young, so I just ended up stuck in the one place all the time. I know John was there in Leeds at the same time as me, but he had his own life: he was courting, he had met his future wife Peggy and I didn't see an awful lot of him. I tried to keep my head up and hoped the football would ease the loneliness I was feeling.

I played with the Leeds intermediates, playing mainly in and around Yorkshire against Rotherham, Barnsley, and the two Sheffield teams and so on, but the football was not enough to take my mind off the homesickness. Because John was John, and had been making great strides with the first team, I think I was already living in the shadow of the name a bit, and the coaching staff at Elland Road expected me just to follow in his footsteps and be the same kind of player. It was great to have a brother like him, but even in those early days you felt almost scared to try and follow him.

There was a lad from Swansea who came up at the same time as me too, and that helped for a while. His name was Mickey McCarthy, and he was only little, but eventually Major Buckley said that he wasn't going to make it as a player with Leeds so he asked if it was okay for me to take him home and make sure he got back safely. So I said 'Yes, Sir, I'll take him home', but as soon as I was on that train towards Swansea it felt like a big weight had been lifted from my shoulders and I knew then I was never coming back. I am sorry if that upset Major Buckley in any way, but sometimes you just get a gut feeling and go with it, and as it turns out it was the right move for me. He was probably disappointed that I had packed it in so unexpectedly, and John was a little surprised too, but as soon as I got back home and saw all my friends and family I knew that I had done the right thing.

I hadn't been long back in Swansea when Joe Sykes came up from the Vetch and said: 'Look, son, why don't you come to the Vetch and join the ground staff at Swansea, stick in and we'll give you thirty bob a week?'. That sounded all right to me and I wasn't exactly awash with ideas about what I was going to do next with my life, so I jumped at the chance. Swansea were still smarting about John slipping through the net and didn't want to make the same mistake twice.

CHAPTER 5
FROM DUCKLING TO SWAN

'When we were firing on all cylinders I would say the Swans could prove a match for anyone on our day, especially in front of a big, passionate crowd at the Vetch.'
MEL CHARLES

BEFORE I WENT FULL-TIME at the Swans I tried my luck as an apprentice refrigeration engineer. Maybe not the ideal career choice and not one I had really been banking on, but the idea of making some money was enough to force me to get my arse into gear and earn some honest cash. Mind you, I only did it for six months. I used to go up to the Valleys, lugging the big bottles in and out of places, and I would get paid six shillings a week for it. But doing some hard graft opened my eyes a little. As well as the fact that it built me up physically it also stood me in good stead as a person. I soon realised there was a big, wide world out there beyond football – and a hard one at that. In football, to a certain extent, everything is done for you and you end up being pampered to a degree. Sometimes you just had to turn up, jump on the bus, stick the boots on and play. Hotels were booked for you, sometimes bills or rent was paid, nothing really worried you. But when you realise guys have to sweat and toil just to make sure they've enough to eat, drink and look after their families, it gives you a reality check and stops you from ever getting big-headed or thinking you're the big noise.

After Leeds, I was back playing local amateur football. I was already completely addicted to the game, and just took the attitude that as long as I was playing, I was not going to get too het up about the level I was at. I was playing centre-forward for the local side Stepney and banging the goals in left, right and centre – I scored seven in one game! Then the Swans came calling, and once again the dream of making it as a professional footballer came closer to becoming a reality. I could have gone to Cardiff at that time, but my dad – who was looking out for me, the way he looked out for John when he had a big decision to make – was told in no uncertain terms there was no money to be made from it, and in his opinion I would be better off going to the Swans. I didn't really need the advice, because when I heard the Swans were interested in me, my heart was set on going to the Vetch anyway. Often when I was feeling down when I was up at Leeds, I thought life would be a lot simpler had I signed instead for Swansea. Now that chance had arrived I didn't need a hell of a lot of persuasion to stay and sign for my home town team.

It was quite a leap to make, though. I went straight from what was basically a pub team playing away in the local leagues to being first on the ground staff, then a professional at 17, and then more or less right into the first team in the Second Division of the Football League. And that was where I stayed. I was young, fit and my legs were strong and unaware of the numerous injuries that would be coming their way in future years. I don't think I ever got dropped for the Swans, and the only time I missed any games was when I had to go under the knife to get my cartilage out.

I didn't know it at the time, but it was the beginning of something of a special time for the Swans. A lot of local lads were being brought through the ranks at the same time, probably because the board knew that blooding young players would be the most cost-efficient way to run a club which was financially a little unstable. And while there were times when we let ourselves down and ultimately cost ourselves promotion to the First Division with some patchy away results, we were a team full of characters and entertainers. We had some great players coming through the ranks, many of whom would be sold on for big fees later down the line. When we were firing on all cylinders I would say we could prove a match for anyone on our day, especially in front of a big, passionate crowd at the Vetch.

There wasn't much money in football in those days and it was a far cry from the glamorous lifestyle it is now. In fact, Cliffy Jones, one of my big mates during my time at the Vetch and a good friend to this day, had to work as a sheet-metal apprentice down the docks while he was a teenager at Swansea Town. His dad reckoned it wouldn't do him any harm to have a trade. It was an era when you would listen to what your father told you – most of the time he would be right, and what we lacked in common sense the old man would often provide. But Cliff tells the story of how he scored the winner against England for Wales one day and was back down the docks at seven the next morning to do his shift, with the foreman telling him, 'Well done lad, but you can get on with your proper work now!' No wonder we didn't get ideas above our station.

My father was just pleased to see me sign for the Swans and it made me feel good to see him happy and proud, watching his son playing for the local team. He was already proud of John, of course, and the rest of the family too, but to see one of his boys run out in the white of Swansea gave him an extra thrill, and it didn't do him any harm when he was in the pub and in need of somebody to buy him a drink either. The punters were probably saying to themselves, 'Oh, there's Mel Charles' dad, his boy plays for the Swans, maybe if I buy him a pint of beer he'll be able to get us a ticket for the Vetch.' And sure enough, my father wouldn't say no to the offer of a beer! He was a real character: he used to walk everywhere and would never be seen on a bus. I used to get two tickets for each game when I played for the Swans, but where I lived there were about 19 pubs going down the road on the way to the Vetch and he would pop in to every one. And in each pub, he would promise people tickets just so they would buy him a pint. He turned up at the ground one day and there they all were – a big gang of folk all waiting for tickets they reckoned they had been promised, 19 of them chasing those two complimentary tickets. He would call me over and say, 'Hey, Mel, any chance of getting a few extra tickets? I promised them I would get them in…' I just remember shaking my head and thinking what a silly old bugger he was. I may have been doing all right, but if the directors found out that I was trying to smuggle extra bodies into the Vetch, way beyond my quota, they would have come down on me like a ton of bricks. Paying punters were like gold-dust to them.

I didn't have the same allergy to public transport that my father had, and I would usually jump on the bus to go to home games at the Vetch. It's not like today, where the players swing into their reserved parking spaces in big BMWs, Mercedes or convertible sports cars. We either headed to the game on foot or by bus. It was good being a footballer, and it gave you a bit of fame around town, but it was still a no-frills livelihood, so you didn't think twice about jumping on the bus to go to the game. But I do remember there was one game when I rolled up at the Vetch on a horse and cart. The bus was so full that it went flying right past my stop. A couple of the players, including Mel Nurse, were on the bus as it rumbled on past me, and I think they just sat there having themselves a good laugh at my startled expression and my bad luck instead of giving the driver a nudge and telling him that I had just missed it. Me being me meant I hadn't really left much time for getting there. I was cutting it fine as usual, and by missing the bus I was in serious danger of not getting to the Vetch in time for the match.

By a stroke of luck there was a rag-and-bone man I knew called Jackie Correy, who came along with his horse and cart, clip-clopping towards me moments after I had watched the back end of the bus disappear out of sight. I wasn't too proud to beg for a lift, and was oblivious to the stick I would get for pulling such a crazy stunt, so I told him in sheer desperation that I was playing at the Vetch Field in an hour and needed to get there as fast as his nag's hooves would carry us. So, I hopped on the back, bouncing up and down on the back of the rag-and-bone cart with my bag and my boots as he clip-clopped slowly along the road. As we approached the streets near the Vetch, a big crowd was already gathering – we were getting close to 30,000 attendances in those days. I watched some of the punters rub their eyes in disbelief as they saw me arrive sprawled out on the back of a rag-and-bone cart, gripping on to my football bag and trying not to fall over the side.

It was incredible what happened in those days. You look at the comparison with players today and what they get done for them, but I had no problem slumming it. I think Nursey was waiting for me in the dressing room to rub it in about me missing the bus, but he just started breaking down with laughter again when I told him about the transport I had commandeered to get me to the game on time. I think I was too travel sick to come back at him with any wisecracks – you try it on the back of one of these carts. Talk about a bumpy ride, my stomach was churning!

During my time at the Swans I mainly played centre-half or right-half, the position which I always preferred, which may come as a surprise. I think most people probably remember me as a centre-forward or centre-half, but I really enjoyed playing right-half, which I think gave me more freedom to play the game the way I like it. I could get up and down the pitch no problem for 90 minutes and developed the habit of popping up in the box at exactly the right time to get on the end of opportunities and I scored a lot of goals from that position. I remember Des Palmer, the centre forward at Swansea, used to get really upset whenever I scored more goals than him. These days, you get team-mates kissing and cuddling each other when they score and making a big show of it, but not Des! Instead of jumping on me and kissing me, he used to come up and kick me on the shins and snarl at me because he said right-halves weren't supposed to score goals and I was making him look bad, and he meant it as well! Des didn't do too badly for goals himself though and was a fairly prolific scorer in his day. He was one of the many Swansea players who would win caps for Wales during his time at the Vetch.

Players in general were so much harder in those days, although there wasn't so much needle between teams on the pitch – players just got on with it, got up and dusted themselves down if they had been fouled. There was none of this rolling about as if you have been shot by a sniper. There was also more of a sporting spirit, but that's not to say that we all behaved like choir boys. There was only one player I ever got really annoyed with and that was Billy Elliott at Sunderland. Yes, I know, you'll be laughing at the name – but this Billy Elliott was certainly no ballet dancer, he was a hard player. We played them in the summer and because I tanned easily and looked quite dark-skinned, he said to me: 'Where are you from, the Congo or something? You shouldn't be playing over here!' That upset me and I got stuck into him for that – not when the referee was looking, of course.

Another incident where I lost my cool a bit involved Roy Saunders, Dean Saunders' dad, who was playing for Liverpool at the time. We played them up at Anfield and he kept kicking me, every chance he got. It just seemed he was out to get me that day. I warned him that if he did it again I would sort it out and when he did clatter me again, I reacted, and the next thing I know the crowd started throwing bananas and all sorts at me! They went crazy and they were not too keen on seeing one of their own players getting some of the rough stuff back from an away player. Roy's a big mate of mine now though, and we still have a laugh about that game. Football was a much harder game then than it is now, but players were not mollycoddled in any way. It would be nice to transport some of today's pampered Premiership players back in a time machine to see how they would have coped – I'll tell you the answer though, they wouldn't have lasted five minutes in the Fifties, they're far too spoiled and soft.

Being a footballer was great fun back then; even if the money wasn't a fraction of what's on offer now, we played with a smile on our faces. We were always having laugh. Sometimes we used to train on the beach down at Oystermouth Road at Swansea and that would always ensure there was plenty of great banter among the lads, and a few practical jokes too. Often we would be sent on the long-distance runs to a place called Black Pill, and almost without fail Ray Daniel and I were the back-markers who were last to make it there. Mel Nurse would always want to be first – there always seemed to be one fitness fanatic in a team and at Swansea Town that was Nursey. For those of us who liked to slack a bit and get away without doing anything too strenuous at training, the sight of Mel, keen as mustard and leading us all a merry dance, would get on your nerves after a while, so one day we decided it was time to teach him a little lesson. One hot, sunny day, when the thought of another gruelling run to Black Pill in scorching sunshine was getting us down, Ray and I got our heads together and hatched a cunning plan. The whole group was sent off on the run, on our own with no trainers around. Ray and I made sure we were just out of sight from where the coaches waved us off and then waited for the Mumbles train to come along. With Mel Nurse already a dot on the landscape, no doubt preparing to be first to the finish line once again, the two of us hopped on the train. Our transport would take us along the same route to Black Pill a lot quicker than Nursey's legs would carry him.

The other passengers probably never knew what to make of us, two sweaty footballers in training gear, giggling like little girls as we tried to stay out of sight and look out for our stop a couple of miles along the road. Off we popped at Black Pill, well before any of the other lads, and just in case we were rumbled, we had a cup of water to throw over ourselves to make it look like we'd knocked our pan in and were dripping with sweat. When Nursey finally reached the end of the run, he was fuming when he saw us both standing there grinning like Cheshire cats! He sees the funny side now though.

Although I could be something of a joker and a chancer when it came to training, I could get away with it during my time at

Swansea. I was a naturally fit lad, and whenever it came to the kind of training I knew that I needed to help my sharpness then I would never hide: I would muck in and knuckle down. I was young and I never felt I had to overdo it at training to give my best in a match on a Saturday.

During the summer months, we used to keep fit by playing cricket. We had a cricket team at the Swans, as most of us loved the game and were pretty decent at it too, and we used to play Glamorgan every close-season in a challenge match. Lenny and Ivor Allchurch and Terry Medwin were all pretty useful cricketers. It was a nice change from football, but by the time the new season came round we were all dying to get the boots back on and play our No. 1 love.

Being a footballer was a good and rewarding life, but hopes of making it to the First Division were frequently dashed. Swansea Town were stuck in the Second Division and we couldn't get out, mainly due to the never-ending handicap of having poor away form. Put anybody in front of us at the Vetch and most of the time we would run all over them. A lot of that was to do with the backing that we got from the crowd, and an equal amount was to do with the fact that most of us were Swansea born and bred. It just seemed to drive you on that bit more when you all grew up in the same place. Some of the lads you were playing alongside you had known since your schooldays and in certain cases it added to some extra telepathic understanding. But, as everyone knows, home form alone is never enough to see you through a season and if you can't back up some solid results on your own patch with a few wins here and there on the road, it soon becomes obvious you're going nowhere fast. Sadly, but not uncommonly, the root of the problem in Swansea's case was probably money – or more accurately the lack of it.

Because the directors had hardly any money and were operating on a shoestring budget, there were occasions when we had to set off early on the morning of an away game. There were no overnight stays and fancy hotels for the Swans in those days. If we were travelling up to grounds in the north of England we had to be up at the crack of dawn to make the coach, and any meals we were lucky enough to have on the way were all a bit hurried and disorganised. The roads then were nothing like they are now – it wasn't a case of flying up the motorway in a luxury coach with hours to spare, time to stretch your legs, relax and soak up the atmosphere and surroundings of the ground you are going to play at; it was all a far cry from that. Instead, we would find ourselves slowly trundling up long and winding uneven roads, always racing against the clock to get to our destination on time. You could see the committee nervously checking their watches and trying to get the driver to put his foot down when they knew they were cutting it too fine.

The situation was so bad that a lot of the time we would have to start getting changed on the bus just to ensure that we were stripped and ready to make it on to the pitch in time for kick-off. What a sight we must have looked to other motorists and onlookers. A so-called professional football team hirpling along in a clapped-out bus, with men stripping down to their smalls and trying to squeeze into their socks, pants and shirts, with not enough room to swing a cat! We probably looked a bit odd at the other end of the journey too, jumping off the bus fully changed with our boots on. Any of the home fans watching us pile off, panic-stricken, must have started fancying their team's chances as soon as they clapped eyes on us in the car park. All that rushing about and leaving it till the last minute didn't exactly constitute the ideal warm-up and most of the time we would literally be caught cold. The home team had been there beforehand, limbering up and ready to get stuck into us long before we showed up. In some games we were 2-0 or 3-0 down before we'd even warmed up, with no way back and the points lost.

On one particularly infamous away trip, on a freezing cold day against Rotherham, we were all thoroughly cold and miserable by the time we got to half time. Their ground, Millmoor, is right down in a big ditch. The cold really bites there, and it was one of those games when I wasn't getting much of the ball and had few chances to run about and get myself warm. My teeth were chattering as we went into the dressing room and everyone was looking to try and get some heat into their bodies. They had one of those lovely big boilers in the middle of the dressing room, with a big pipe sticking out of it coming from the wall. A few of the lads were trying to huddle round the boiler, but I thought I would be clever and decided that I was going to get my jersey nice and warm for the second half. I took it off and wrapped it round the pipe, so it would be toasting hot, but I got distracted by the half-time team talk and everything else that was going on in the dressing room and the next thing I knew I started to sense the unmistakable smell of burning. All the lads were looking at each other, wondering where the smell was coming from, and then it finally dawned on me – my bloody jersey was on fire! I grabbed it off the boiler, hoping to limit the damage and my embarrassment as they all started having a laugh at my expense. But there was already a big scorch mark on the white shirt and a dirty great hole burnt clean through the middle. While the manager had been giving the team-talk and I had been dreaming of a nice warm strip to pull on when we went back out for the second half, it had caught fire. I think they would have happily sent me out there with no top on as punishment, but instead we had to hastily borrow a spare jersey from the Rotherham kit room for the second-half. I got some stick from the boys for that one, all the way home as it happens.

We might have had a lot of laughs on the road, but we were all deadly serious when it came to our football. The laughing and joking would stop when we were out there trying to get a result, home or away. We had a great team, with top-notch players like Ivor Allchurch, Cliffy Jones, Lenny Allchurch and Terry Medwin, all of whom were eventually punted on for big transfer fees when they became saleable assets in the eyes of the directors – the Swans used to make a lot of money out of selling their best players, me included when I went to Arsenal.

Ivor Allchurch was a terrific player, and out of all the players who were sold on, he probably managed to stay with Swansea the longest before he too left and joined Newcastle United. Because of his golden locks, he was known as the 'Golden Boy' of Welsh football and he was a big favourite with the team, the fans and the press, all with good reason. Graceful and skilful, he could score goals for fun. He ended up banging in more than 160 goals for the Swans and I think that record stands to this day. Ivor was one of those players who was a joy to play with. Not only did I play alongside him for the Swans and Wales, I would also go on to be in the same side as him at Cardiff, then Haverfordwest in the Welsh League when we were both knocking on a bit in terms of our football careers. While I would say John was the best player I ever played alongside, and not just because he was my brother, Ivor would be right up there with the best too, especially during our time together at the Vetch when we were both probably in the best form of our lives. Mind you, for all his brilliance, I don't think I ever saw Ivor head a ball. He had a touch of class, but I'd be surprised if he ever headed a ball in his life. It was that blond hair of his, I reckon – he didn't want to dirty it!

Ivor's little brother Len, who played on the left wing, was a top player too and he proved to be a great servant to the Swans. He played between 1950 and 1961, and went back and had a second spell too in the early Seventies. Len was at the World Cup with us as part of the Wales squad in Sweden and although he didn't get a game at the finals, he was always a dependable guy to have in the side. He probably felt a bit like me in that he was in the shadow of Ivor to an extent, but what cracking players they both were.

There were lots of good guys around at Swansea and I enjoyed every game I played there. Immaterial of whether we won or lost, I was just glad I was playing. I savoured every minute of it and the first manager I had at the club – Billy McCandless – liked me too, which helped.

I made my debut for Swansea as a 17-year-old at centre-half up at Bramall Lane against Sheffield United, five days before Christmas in 1952, although we got a real going over and lost seven goals. Len Browning was playing that day – the same player whose boots I used to clean when I was at Leeds. He had just joined Sheffield United from Leeds not long before that game. I remember him coming up to me at the end of the match and giving me a warm handshake, even though the look in his eye suggested he really wanted to say: 'Nice to see you've made it, but you've still got a lot to learn, son.'

But I reckon the highlight of my first season would have to be when we beat Leeds – with John in their side – 3-2 at the Vetch. The board of directors were already starting to feel the pinch financially and I suppose that's how I got my big break that season, along with quite a few of the other local lads. McCandless had basically been told that he wouldn't be getting a transfer kitty for signing seasoned pros, so he had to make do with the young blood in the team. So that's what he did: he pitched us in hoping us young Swans would swim not sink, and to be fair I think we all did pretty well. We were keen as mustard and our enthusiasm gave the team a lift. Cliffy was also handed his debut that season, just before me, and he too was just 17, while another lad John Dewsbury, who was a little bit older, was also thrown in at the deep end.

The board did get a few quid to add to their coffers though when we drew Newcastle away in the FA Cup. The game was up at St James' Park and more than 60,000 were in the ground before kick-off, only for it to be called off due to the fog on the Tyne. But they managed to play it a few days later and again the crowd was about 60,000. They doubled their money because there were no refunds for the supporters then, but unfortunately a tidy sum from the gate receipts was all they had to show for the trip because we lost the replayed tussle 3-0.

There really was a strong family feel to the club, and little wonder, because there were times when we had three sets of brothers turning out for us. You can imagine what it was like whenever one of them got kicked – the other brother would jump straight in to his sibling's defence. It could be like the school playground at times. There was Ivor and Len Allchurch, Bryn and Cliff Jones, and Cyril and Gilbert Beech. It's just a shame that John still hadn't been on the Swans' books at that time or we could have been the fourth pair of Swansea siblings. The team also included players like Harry Griffiths, who would go on to become Jeremy's manager at the Swans in the 1970s, Tom Kiley and Terry Medwin, so there was no shortage of class and we were a pretty tasty outfit.

We were prospering fast, and trainers Frank Barson and Joe Sykes were a big influence on us all, particularly Joe who became a real mentor to us. He was the one who would work with us on a day-to-day basis, spot little things in our game that he could work on, and he also had a good manner with the young guys in the squad. Joe knew how to get the best out of you, and that was usually by treating you like an adult and an equal. He was a really good guy, Joe, and I was very grateful for what he did in terms of developing me as a player. Joe had been the first to take an interest in me when I got homesick and came back from Leeds, and when I was playing local league football, he was on the touchline watching me. He was the one who pushed for me to be taken on by the Swans and I appreciated that, especially after he suffered a bad experience in losing John to Leeds.

Joe had been a good player himself for Sheffield Wednesday and played more than 300 games for the Swans, and he was like a father to us at times. He was a lovely fellow, but I have to say that all the coaching staff at the Vetch were nice people and a tremendous help. The captain, Billy Lucas, also played a big part in helping me grow up as a footballer. He was probably the best signing Billy McCandless ever made, and it was just as well because the £11,000 they paid for him in 1947 was a club record at the time!

Billy Lucas was the complete player: he was one of those guys who was able to read the game inside out and he was happy to share his knowledge with the younger players in the team. He took me under his wing on the pitch when we were playing alongside each other, and when I was playing centre-half and he was right-half, he would talk me through the game. Billy would tell you when to release the ball, when to run into space and how to mark. I knew immediately how lucky I was to be playing next to somebody with that kind of experience, who was willing to go out of his way to help you. You appreciate it and make sure you don't waste the opportunity of learning everything that's being passed on.

McCandless also played his part, of course, and he was often being urged by the board to take as active a role in training as possible to ensure we were all handled properly and to help us develop as players. They wanted him to take a hands-on role and he would come down to training and sit on a bench and watch us being put through our paces. He wasn't really one for tactics, though. Very few managers were in those days and they didn't have the same obsession with man-marking and trying to cancel out opponents the way they do now. The philosophy was a simple one – just go out there and play your own game. Don't spend your time obsessing about the team you are playing against or you won't be able to express yourselves. This may sound a bit naïve and simplistic, but when you were dealing with a bunch of young players just eager to go out there and put on a show for the fans, then it wasn't a bad approach and most of the time it worked. But there was definitely an awareness at boardroom level that we were a precocious bunch, and if handled in the wrong way, we could end up being burnt out too early. They knew they had some good young players on their hands, and if we were nurtured along in the right way we would ensure a bright and prosperous future for Swansea.

CHAPTER 6
ARMY MANOEUVRES

*'I enjoyed the Army because I would play football in the autumn,
winter and spring, then cricket in the summer; it was like a
Butlin's holiday camp at times.'*
MEL CHARLES

IT WAS GREAT BEING a Swansea lad and playing for the local team – you felt like you were the big noise about town whenever you went out. If you were out at weekends you could stroll straight to the front of the queue at the dancing. The doormen would just wave you to the front. People recognised you and it was a good feeling; your chest would be puffed out with pride. We would rub shoulders with all the big faces who were out and about in the town, and of course we would always get a bit of extra attention from the girls too, which was an added bonus. But there was a hiccup on the horizon in my football career – I had to do my bit for the Army and my early days as a Swansea Town player coincided with my short, but eventful, National Service.

As I mentioned, I was never really one for sticking in at school and wasn't great at doing what I was told. I had the attention span of a goldfish and I think I had an allergy to rules and regulations. My aversion to authority always seemed to get me into a few scrapes. So the thought of National Service didn't exactly fill me with glee. Don't get me wrong, I was happy enough to do it because the War was still fresh in people's minds and you saw a lot of brave old soldiers living in town who had fought for their country and I had nothing but admiration for them. I was also proud of the part my dad had played in the Armed Forces. For that reason, it didn't seem like they were asking too much for me to do my bit for the Armed Forces and do a couple of years of National Service.

When I first went to enlist in Swansea I told them that ideally I wanted to be in the Navy, just as my dad had been, but they wouldn't let me. Because I was a footballer they said I had to enlist in the Army. I don't know the reason for that, but I think it allowed you to more or less continue playing for your club, whereas if you were stuck on a big ship floating in the ocean somewhere it wouldn't be too handy for nipping back to play football, would it? John had already done his National Service during his time at Leeds, and he was based up at Catterick, and lots of other footballers throughout the divisions were forced to do the same. The truth, is everybody did it without the slightest grumble. The Army was very accommodating and did all it could to make sure that you could fit your time as a soldier in around your football career, and thankfully that meant that you did not necessarily have to put your football on hold. At first I didn't really like the sound of the Army and had horrible visions of it involving a lot of marching and plenty of hard graft, which was definitely not up my street in those days. However, I reluctantly went ahead and did my stint, although the way it worked out my short time in uniform was all about football, rather than life as a common soldier.

Unfortunately, one thing that was unavoidable was the 'square-bashing' on the parade ground which followed soon after you signed up. This was the basic Army training which is compulsory for any new recruit, and I got my square-bashing down in Aldershot. Bloody hopeless I was! There was this big, loud terrifying Sergeant Major shouting and screaming at us at the top of his voice, and every time he bellowed I would be all over the place. I must have looked a proper Charlie, getting all the instructions wrong. I probably looked like Clive Dunn in *Dad's Army*, except a younger, dafter version. You would think I might have some kind of co-ordination as a footballer, having gone through a few training drills with the Swans, but not a bit of it. This was completely alien to me and the louder he shouted the more I seemed to mess it up. I was left looking like a spare part as I scurried backwards and forwards trying to keep up with the orders he was bellowing towards me. In his eyes, I definitely was an ''orrible little man'. I think it was just the sheer terror of his voice that was putting me off my stride. If he wanted me to go left, I would go right; if he wanted me to go forwards, I would go backwards – I was all over the place. I think he just had me marked down as a lost cause and by the end of it, he was telling me to get out the way as I was cramping the style of some of the other recruits. They were all grateful to me though, because at least I was making them look good and giving them a few laughs into the bargain, although you were meant to keep a stiff upper lip, which was hard with me around.

Mercifully, the square-bashing was as hard as it ever got for me as a soldier, and I use the word loosely, because six weeks later they sent me to the Army base at Donington in Shropshire. I was assigned to the Royal Army Ordnance Corps (RAOC), which dealt with the supply of weapons and munitions and Army equipment.

For me, this was to prove more like a holiday camp than a military one. I ended up becoming the sergeant, in charge of camp staff, but I really didn't have to do any of the dirty work; the other lads did this most of the time and I was given a free rein to do as I pleased. It didn't take long for it to dawn on me that I was being singled out for some special treatment because I was a footballer. It was soon apparent I had been cherry-picked for the 9th Battalion RAOC by the Brigadier, who happened to be football-mad. He was called Brigadier Snooks and I think he later became a director of Wolverhampton Wanderers. While he clearly enjoyed his life as an Army officer, he was a cunning old fox and was desperate to ensure that his football side was the best in the Armed Forces. I can imagine it gave him a lot of pride when he discussed his team's achievements in the Officers' Mess. It turned out he had been carefully sifting through the recruitment papers from all over the country, picking out players here and there, and had started assembling a side that would be able to challenge strongly for football honours within the Armed Forces, which always carried a lot of prestige.

I wasn't the only footballer in the battalion, and that was no accident. I played with the England international right-half Eddie Clamp and his Wolves team-mates Peter Russell and Colin Booth, the goalkeeper John Hollowbread of Tottenham Hotspur and Ron 'Chips' Rafferty of Grimsby Town. There were a couple of other lads who played for Portsmouth – we had a great side. We had Phil Woosnam in the team too and he was a lieutenant. Phil was a good inside forward for West Ham and won quite a few caps for Wales. They had all come from good clubs. Wolves, in particular, were a really strong team back then and won First Division league titles not long after our stint in the Army, so it gives you some idea of the level of player we had within our battalion.

In my two years there the 9th Battalion RAOC won everything there was to win. I was able to visit Germany, Belgium and France to play in Army matches and closer to home we would go up to Catterick to play other teams within the British Army, also packed with professionals doing their National Service. Although I was still playing as a right-half with Swansea, I was playing centre forward for the Army and loving every moment of it. I scored more than 100 goals in my two years with the 9th Battalion. If you had given me a rifle I probably couldn't have shot straight to save my life, but when it came to firing the ball into the back of the net I was one of the sharpest shots in the Army.

We took the football seriously and always tried to win everything we entered. We were, after all, doing our National Service during peace time and to be honest, everybody was glad that football gave us something to focus on. The British Cup competitions were the most exciting and the whole camp would be buzzing whenever we had a big game coming up. We played the Engineers in the semi-final of the Army Cup and won 2-1, and I will never forget the final at Aldershot's ground, where we were losing 3-1 at half-time against the Army Catering Corps. I was the captain, and I saw the Brigadier coming over to me to have a word. I thought he was going to give me a rocket for our shoddy display in the first half and threaten me that all my privileges would be taken away, but instead he went for bit of reverse psychology. He was a fairly gentle bloke anyway, but very intelligent with it, and he always had the knack of managing to get through to you with a few well-chosen words rather than barking orders in the way that some of the sergeants would. So he came over and put an arm round my shoulder, taking the softly-softly approach, and said to me: 'Well, Mel, you've done your job. You've given me a lot of satisfaction by getting us to the Army Cup final and I must thank you for that.' It felt like he was giving up and was prepared to settle for second best, and that got my adrenaline pumping. The thought of us having made it this far and having to settle for being runners-up was enough to get me fired up for the second half so I yelled at him: 'The game's not over yet!'

His subtle mind games worked a treat on me and I went out and scored a hat-trick. It was real Roy of the Rovers stuff; everything came off for me perfectly in that second-half. The Brigadier must have known full well that he would be able to get inside my head and he knew exactly what buttons to press to secure the response that he was looking for. With the cup ready to take pride of place in the regimental trophy cabinet I became something of a hero in the Brigadier's eyes and I was sent home on a fortnight's leave as a reward – happy days!

We managed to see a bit of the world, too, and our tour of Germany was extremely interesting, even if it was really just a jolly for us to play a series of football matches as the Army Cup champions. We travelled from Dortmund through Hanover, right round the country, and we did well out there. It was weird being out there with the Army because the last time they had been there they had been fighting the Germans, not playing football against them. It was a good experience though, and every day brought a new adventure.

The football team went everywhere and led a privileged life in the Army. I probably shouldn't say this but it was like a holiday camp. Mind you, I agree with the idea of having National Service and they probably should have kept it going. It does teach discipline and I think it would solve a lot of the problems today, giving youngsters some focus and structure. When you're in the Army you've got to pay attention and while it was easy for me, the experience still taught me some good lessons in life. I enjoyed it because I would play football in the autumn, winter and spring and then cricket in the summer – it was like a Butlin's holiday camp at times. I didn't miss many games for the Swans though and I remember there was one time I pulled a bit of a fast one when I came back to Wales for a weekend from the Army to play for them. We were playing up at Port Vale in an away match, but because I hadn't been home to Swansea for ages I pretended I thought the match was at the Vetch, headed back home on the train and then acted like I had been the unwitting victim of a dreadful mix-up. By the time I got to Swansea it was far too late to make a quick dash up to the Potteries to join up with the first team, so they told me they would have to make do without me and that I would just have to turn out for the reserves in the Combination instead. I hadn't been home for 12 weeks so I was well chuffed to get away with that one. It didn't bother me too much that I had missed the Swans' game up at Port Vale; I suppose I was just missing home too much and wanted a bit of my mother's cooking.

We won the Army Cup both years that I was there and I was still allowed to go and play for the Swans almost whenever I wanted. I used to go home on the weekend and return to the base on a Monday. There was train that went right through mid-Wales to Shrewsbury. I used to catch it at quarter to eight on a Monday and then just stroll back into camp. The Army base was a happy place though and we all got on well together. We would spend our evenings playing table tennis and sitting and chatting. There was great camaraderie among us all and I think the football made for an even stronger unit.

I don't know if we would have made crack soldiers had another war kicked off, though, because our heads were full of football instead of fighting. There wasn't even the class divide you might expect between the common soldiers and the officers. Even the top brass would tip me the wink from time to time – they knew they would have to answer to the Brigadier otherwise, because the football team always came first in his eyes. The Army was a fantastic time for me, but I was on duty when I developed my first knee problem, aged only 18. It was a stupid way to get injured too. I would like to say I got the injury steaming into a tackle in a match, but the truth was that it was self-inflicted and I actually did all the damage after coming out of the cookhouse. I was just strolling out, my head in the clouds, when somebody kicked a ball at me and I instinctively took a swipe at it and missed, twisting my knee in the process. That was typical of me, really – acting daft! I didn't know it at the time, but it was to prove the first of many knee injuries and both knees still give me serious gyp to this day. I was quite lucky with injuries over the piece though; I think I only had that one serious injury during my time at Swansea, the same one I managed to inflict on myself with the fresh-air kick I attempted coming out of the Army cookhouse. But my luck was to run out later in my career when I became a regular on the treatment table, and ask any player: the treatment table is a depressing place to be.

But most of the time I was able to look after myself and steer clear of the physio's room. And because I was staying fit, I was able to hold down my place in the first team and rack up a lot of appearances. In fact, other than the time I ducked out of the trip to Port Vale, I think I only played once in the second team in the Combination, and that was just after I had my cartilage operation on my knee. I was itching to get back into the first team as soon as was humanly possible and I stated my case by scoring five goals in that game, against Swindon. For some peculiar reason, I seemed to make a habit of scoring goals against Swindon. I think most players probably find that – there are certain teams that you always do well against for some reason, and other sides that end up being bogey teams for you personally. But in that game against Swindon, Graham Davis was on the wing, slinging the crosses in, and I was getting on the end of everything, nodding them into the net.

Graham was a good pal of mine and it was a shame for him during his time at the Vetch because although he was a tidy player, no matter what he did in the second team, he couldn't get into the first team because there was Lenny Allchurch on one wing and Ivor Allchurch on the other, and those two never seemed to get injured. It was impossible for poor Davo to get in. He was doing well in the Combination but he just couldn't get in the first team. It was difficult sometimes when you had mates that came and went from the Swans, but there were only 11 places up for grabs on a Saturday, with no substitutes, so only the very best made it, and if you had an international ahead of you in the pecking order, it was tough. I was one of the lucky ones, but once I was in that first team, my view was that there was no way that I was going to surrender my place to anyone.

CHAPTER 7

JACK-OF-ALL-TRADES

'The directors were only interested in keeping the accountants happy by raking in some tidy transfer fees, and building a team and keeping it together was of secondary importance.'
MEL CHARLES

SWANSEA TOWN MANAGER Billy McCandless was old enough and experienced enough to know that when you've got a team of young kids there's going to be the odd sticky spell. He also knew that it was important that when the inevitable setbacks arrived we reacted in the right way and didn't get too disheartened. When you're young and a little bit wet behind the ears, if you're able to string a few good results together then you start taking it for granted that everything is going to run smoothly. An element of cockiness creeps into your game. Only with experience do you learn that football is a game of ups and downs, and has a habit of biting you on the backside when you least expect it. In time, though, you realise that you've got to learn how to take the rough with the smooth.

I remember we got a particularly harsh lesson in football at the beginning of the 1953/54 season when we were thrashed 6–0 by Birmingham. We were lost for words and left completely dejected afterwards in the dressing room. I don't think any of us had ever experienced a hammering like it, and our spirits needed nursing back to health a bit on the training ground after that débâcle. This would turn out to be a very tough season because the board were starting to become obsessed with the balance sheet, as I suppose they were entitled to do if it wasn't making pleasant reading. We only really heard the vibes from the boardroom through the grapevine, but we knew that the club wasn't exactly flush with cash. You just had to take one look round the place to see that. The club sold on good players like Arthur Morgan and Frank Scrine, and nobody was coming in the other way. More and more responsibility was being placed on our young shoulders and the balance of the team was starting to look a little lop-sided, leaving us vulnerable in matches where experience could be the difference between winning and losing. We almost went down that year, and that gave the directors more of a fright than anything. They reacted by snapping up Ron Burgess on a free transfer from Spurs as player-coach, and he got us moving back in the right direction. Arthur Willis, an experienced full-back, was also signed and we started to play some stylish, uninhibited football, which the fans appreciated.

Because we were such an attacking team, we were guilty of leaving ourselves open at the back far too often and on the occasions where the forwards and half-backs couldn't stamp their authority on a game, we were often on the end of some heavy defeats, usually on the road. I remember we were once given the incentive of a bumped-up bonus of £5 if we won a match at Huddersfield, and having the carrot of a little extra cash dangled in front of us did the trick – I think we won 4-0, and that was when they had a skinny little teenager called Denis Law in the team and the great Bill Shankly as their manager. I'm not saying that we went out there and tried harder just because we were being offered more money, but it certainly made us focus on the game and it was a good feeling to know that we had earned ourselves a few extra pennies for our pockets through a real team effort. The beers tasted much, much better that night, I can tell you!

For every bad defeat that we suffered away from home, we had some resounding wins too, usually in front of an appreciative crowd at the Vetch, where the crowds were really good, nudging 30,000 sometimes. The fans streamed through the turnstiles when word got round that a team of young local lads was playing with a bit of style. We were happy to go out there and entertain them, and between myself, Ivor, Cliffy, Terry Medwin and Harry Griffiths, we scored a pile of goals.

After staying up on that occasion by the tightest of margins, we were thrown into turmoil before a ball was even kicked in the 1955/56 season when Billy McCandless suddenly died. It's a sad enough time when somebody close to a football club dies, and it puts the game into perspective, but when it's your manager too there's a bit of added uncertainty. The board did the sensible thing by keeping his successor in-house and gave the job to Ron Burgess, with Ivor and Joe Sykes also there to give him a helping hand on the training ground.

The style of football under Ron was still geared towards attack, especially at home, and I was getting a lot of goals from my favourite position of right-half. Our ability to entertain was the talk of Swansea, and when we played Leeds at the Vetch they had to shut the gates half an hour before kick-off – there were already 30,000 punters inside and they couldn't squeeze any more in! That one ended up a draw, but most of those crammed in like sardines on the North Bank would be back week in, week out, and it was their support that helped spur us on to plenty more victories at home. We were top of the league for a while that season and were playing out of our skins, but the Swans being the Swans, we just couldn't stay at the top.

The rot set in a bit when Tom Kiley got a bad injury, and that upset the team's form a bit, and we ended up sliding back to our familiar mid-table position. A season which had promised an awful lot, including the tantalising prospect of promotion to the First Division, just faded tamely away in the end. And just when we thought it couldn't get any worse, it did, because the club decided to sell Terry Medwin to Spurs. We didn't know it at the time, but quite a few more of us would be following Terry out of the exit door in the years to come, with little effort to stop us made by the club. It seemed the directors were only interested in keeping the accountants happy by raking in some tidy transfer fees, and building a team and keeping it together was of secondary importance. Around that time they put up a roof over the North Bank at the Vetch, but this was more down to the generosity of the club's loyal fans than anything else. The Swans Supporters Club paid for that and handed over a cheque for £16,000 to meet the costs, which was a marvellous gesture and a huge amount of cash in those days. That was the kind of club we were, though. Everyone pulled together whatever way they could and there was a proper sense of the club belonging to the community. There were always enough Swansea lads in the team to ensure that we provided maximum effort on the pitch to repay the support we were getting from the terraces.

Most of the time, I was enjoying the chance to play in my favourite position of right-half, and because we had so many goalscorers in the side I think the role ideally suited me. I was mainly right footed, but I was always looking to get on the end of high balls and scored a lot of goals with my head; I suppose I was pretty fearless and a lot of the time I would be happy to stick my head where others might not fancy putting their boot. But I don't know if that attitude was brave or stupid, because I remember breaking my nose against Stoke at the Vetch in a cup tie. The goalkeeper who did this to me was Wilf Hall. He had been in the Army with me, but there were no hard feelings. It was a ball we were both entitled to go for and on that occasion it was me who came off second best. You know what they say about goalkeepers anyway – they are all crazy, and it was probably no surprise that he was out to make damn sure he wasn't going to lose out to me when we jumped for the ball.

I got on well with Wilf and later in my career, when I played for Port Vale, I would run into him again. There were a lot of opponents that you would come up against who you liked and respected, and while you were never quite bosom buddies, if you ran into each other in future years there was always the chance for a word and a quick catch-up after the game. Of course there were others you would avoid like the plague, but they were few and far between because by and large, footballers were a decent bunch of blokes in the Fifties and Sixties. The vast majority of us came from working-class backgrounds and had worked hard to get to where we were, so there were no airs and graces, and very few egos. Even the top British internationals were generally level-headed guys, and there was no room for big-heads – they would have soon found themselves ostracised by their team-mates. There were certainly no egos to be massaged at Swansea – we were a working-class team for working-class people and we all liked it that way.

Some other early memories from my days at Swansea Town included my first hat-trick as a Swan against Llanelli in the Welsh Cup, and then a run to the Welsh Cup final in the 1955/56 season. We'd beaten Newport County easily enough in the semi-final, but unfortunately we came up short in the final and lost to Cardiff 3-2. It was disappointing to lose, but with the Welsh Cup there was always the feeling that we would quickly gain the chance to win it next time round, whereas with the FA Cup you knew just how difficult it was to get any kind of run going.

The 1956/57 season saw us swing from one extreme to the other. We banged in 90 goals in the league with some breathtaking cavalier football. The only problem was that we managed to *concede* 90 as well! Because I was, by this stage, being switched back and forth between centre-forward and centre-half a lot, you could say I had a helping hand in both these sets of statistics! I got my share of goals though, whether I was playing up front, at right-half or at the back. There was even one game against Fulham when our goalkeeper Johnny King, who was something of a Swans legend, ended up playing at centre forward after he became injured in a 4-4 draw. The fans certainly got their money's worth when they came down to the Vetch. We were entertainers all right!

I played against John a few times when he was still at Leeds and there was a nice picture taken of the two of us shaking hands before the 1956 league game at Elland Road. While the Swans could occasionally send out three sets of brothers in the same side, that game had the distinction of having three sets of brothers between the two teams – which must be some kind of record unless the Jackson Five ever played a charity match against the

Osmonds! As well as John and me, there was Len and Ivor Allchurch and Cliffy and Bryn Jones. Leeds were on a 32-game unbeaten run in the league going into that game, but we weren't a side for respecting reputations and we came mighty close to turning them over that day. The only reason they managed to peg us back to a 2-2 draw was because we had to play most of the second half with ten men because Bryn Jones was injured.

It's safe to say the Charles brothers were enjoying the added spice of playing against each other and there were definitely big bragging rights at stake. It was John who struck the first blow when he scored a penalty, his 100th league goal for Leeds. But I wasn't having him stealing all the glory and I was delighted that it was me who grabbed the equaliser for Swansea. I remember giving him a cheeky grin as I ran back towards the halfway line after that goal, and I think he saw the funny side of his little brother trying to get one over on him. It was like a throwback to one of our childhood fights, but this time with forty-odd thousand watching us. Ivor Allchurch put us 2-1 up, but we just couldn't hold on with the ten men and had to settle for a point when we had deserved what would have been a famous win.

I was getting a lot of goals for the Swans, a part of my game that was important to me, as I always got a thrill out of scoring. In those days I got a few hat-tricks too, although that was long before you tried to swipe the match ball as a souvenir. The club simply couldn't afford it. If you'd have tried to sneak the ball out of the stadium, they would have been chasing you down the road to get you to hand it back. They were the big heavy leather balls in those days, not the lightweight efforts you see now, and they must have cost a few bob, so hat-trick or not there was no way they were going to hand over match balls when a pat on the back would suffice.

After my Welsh Cup hat-trick against Llanelli, I scored four in the opening game of the 1956/57 season against Blackburn, a hat-trick against Stoke the next season, then another two hat-tricks the season after that against Middlesbrough and Sheffield Wednesday. It was always a great feeling to score a hat-trick and after you had two goals under your belt in the one game there was always the extra motivation to go on and try and get a third, without being greedy – there were certain team-mates who would have lynched you afterwards, had you tried to grab all the glory yourself at the expense of the team.

A Welsh Cup winner's medal was to elude me again in the 1956/57 season. To reach the final, we battled our way past our old cup foes Newport County, who must have been sick of the sight of us in those days, although it took us a replay, which we won 3-0 at the Vetch. Cardiff had been knocked out too and when we came up against Wrexham in the final we really fancied our chances of lifting the trophy at Ninian Park. Maybe we fancied them a little too much, because we struggled in the role of hot favourites and never played anything like our best, and deservedly lost 2-0. For a free-scoring team, it was very much out of character for us to draw a blank, but we just didn't perform and the cup was heading up to north Wales instead of to the Vetch. We were in the midst of a bit of a drought in the competition, and maybe we just felt the pressure a bit too much, knowing that the Swans had last won the Welsh Cup in 1950. By the time it finally had our white ribbons on it again in the 1960/61 season, I was off to pastures new and that is something I regret. Sadly I would never win the trophy as a Swansea player, but I would get my hands on the elusive cup later in my career.

I never got far with my dreams in the FA Cup, but the cup adventures I had were enjoyable during my time at the Vetch, even if they were, for the most part, short-lived. We lost up at Newcastle in my first season, then Everton the next year, but the 1954/55 season saw us go on a decent run. We started off with a good win away to Blackburn, then we played out of our skins to beat Stoke City 3-1 at the Vetch. They were a really good side then and it was an excellent scalp for us to take.

The Fifth Round tie against Sunderland saw the Vetch at its very best – packed to the rafters with the fans roaring us on every step of the way. It wasn't quite enough to lift us past what was an excellent Sunderland team though, and we were held to a 2-2 draw. Our best chance of making it through to the quarter-finals had gone, and though we put up a good fight at Roker Park, we lost 1-0 in the replay. The seasons after that saw Swansea fall at the first hurdle every time – first York City, then Wolves, Burnley and Portsmouth. The Swans went on to have a famous run in 1964 though, again sadly after I was away, beating Liverpool on the way to the semi-finals before they got knocked out by Preston North End at Villa Park. I was long gone by then, and would have loved to have been involved in a cup run like that, but the FA Cup was never really particularly kind to me. I suppose it's only the lucky few who get to experience the magic of the cup, although you always had a sense of how special it was, even in the early rounds, and there was an edge to every tie. The players loved it, the fans loved it, the directors loved it – especially whenever a big gate receipt came their way. The FA Cup has been described as the greatest club football competition in the world and although I never had the honour of getting near a final myself, I would agree with that. It was unique and it's good to see that in this day and age it is still producing fairytales year in, year out.

Towards the end of my time at the Vetch, my form was good, but it was an unsettling period at the club. Every week, there seemed to be rumours about players leaving, me included, with Newcastle and Manchester United supposedly interested in signing me, and Arsenal and Tottenham also said to be watching me. The word was that I was up for sale, and the club had been putting out feelers to the clubs in the First Division because they knew that was the only place where they were going to get the kind of fee that they were after for me.

It took a while before it reached the stage where I handed in an official transfer request, but the board were making it quite clear that they didn't see my long-term future at Swansea. I would have gladly stayed at the club, had we come to a decent financial agreement, but if that was the attitude they were going to take, then I at least had to keep an open mind to where I would be heading next. Every week there seemed to be a new team linked with me and I couldn't go anywhere in town without somebody asking me where I was heading, but I just had to shrug my shoulders and say that I had heard nothing concrete. And while I admit that it was all unsettling and that I was starting to get itchy feet at the Swans, I never did hear of any definite interest first-hand, it was all innuendo and paper talk. If I'd been given a pound for every rumour that was doing the rounds then, I would have been able to retire on the spot.

It got to the stage where there were so many wild stories flying about that I just decided to say nothing at all about all the speculation and maybe that was the wrong thing to do. Sometimes if you decide on that approach people automatically think that you are hiding something. But anybody who knew me was aware that wasn't my style. I would like to think I was always honest and while I have as many flaws and faults as the next man, honesty was never a problem for me. The truth of the matter was that I just wanted to concentrate on playing football for Swansea Town and I saw anything else as a distraction that might affect my form.

But I wasn't the only player on our books going through all that, far from it. One week, the big rumour or headline would be about me, then another week it would be Cliffy, then it was Ivor's turn and so it went on. The newspaper men would keep on asking me what was happening, but I just used to shrug it off and say I didn't know anything – the truth was I knew as much as them… nothing.

The off-the-field nonsense probably affected our form that season, but despite all the unrest and some very poor results we were still capable of producing the odd moment of magic at the Vetch. One game that sticks in the mind is when we thumped Derby County 7-0. It wasn't long before the World Cup, and although we had seven Welsh internationals in the squad and had started the season being tipped by a lot of people to win promotion, instead we found ourselves in deep, deep relegation trouble and facing the unthinkable prospect of relegation to Division Three. That could have put a real downer on the trip to the World Cup for the Wales players involved – who knows, maybe we would have been playing under a cloud and been unable to raise ourselves to the heights that we did in Sweden. It would have been hanging over us, knowing that when the finals were over we would be coming back to the third division.

We had lost a few games going into the Derby County match, folk were starting to get twitchy, and Ron Burgess had been trying to get the fans whipped up into giving us their full backing from the North Bank – and boy, we never let them down – they were behind us from the start and they were like a twelfth man. Ivor banged in a hat-trick and Ray Daniel and I also got on the scoresheet as we ran riot. I think there had been a lot of pent-up frustration about the way we had let ourselves down that season and under-achieved, so we just took all that anger out on Derby and showed the kind of football we were capable of producing when everyone was firing on all cylinders. That 7-0 rout was just the boost we needed, and although we had to beat Bristol City away on the last day of the season, we were so determined to stay up that we didn't let the opportunity pass us by. We never felt any nerves and were remarkably focused from the first whistle, just sensing it was our destiny we would stay up. We comfortably won 2-1 and the Welsh caps in the side were able to go to Sweden with one less thing to worry about.

There was another game the following season where we actually managed to field an all-Welsh international side in Swansea colours – eight full caps and three youth caps. The historic team that took the field that day was John King, Dai Thomas, Harry Griffiths, Brian Hughes, Mel Nurse, Malcolm Kennedy, Len Allchurch, Reg Davies, Mel Charles, Des Palmer and Colin Webster.

I think there were a dozen Swansea players who won international caps in the Fifties, more than in than any other decade in the club's history, and it really was an incredible time for not only producing home-grown players, but special ones at that. Among the players capped by Wales during their time at Swansea were myself, Ivor and Len Allchurch, Jim Feeney, Jack Parry, Harry Griffiths, Terry Medwin, Cliff Jones, John King, Des Palmer, Dai Thomas and Mel Nurse.

It would have been great to keep all those players together but it was never going to happen at Swansea, partly because a lot of us were destined for bigger things, but mainly because the transfer fees commanded by us would keep the club going. The big First Division teams were constantly keeping tabs on our players because they knew that Wales were a tidy international side and I think they probably thought they could pick us up at rock-bottom prices too, which definitely wasn't the case. The board of directors at Swansea were a canny lot and wouldn't roll over for anyone when it came to sitting round the table and negotiating transfer fees.

I remember we played Manchester United in a friendly at the Vetch and after I scored a couple of goals in an amazing match which we lost 6-4, I saw Matt Busby in the paper quoted afterwards saying: 'I want to sign Mel'. I was quite excited until I found out that he meant Mel Nurse instead!

A career at Old Trafford would have done me nicely, although in the end he didn't sign Nursey either as he went on to sign for Middlesbrough instead. That game was played the year after the Munich air disaster and we fixed it up on a weekend when neither team was involved in the FA Cup. The proceeds went to charity and the fans were treated to one hell of a game – ten goals, and it was none of your exhibition stuff: both teams wanted to win and we served up a brilliant match. I think it was one of Albert Quixall's first games after he signed from Sheffield Wednesday for what was a record transfer fee at the time of £45,000. My fee when I signed for Arsenal was around the same, but with two players thrown in for good measure, which made my transfer the most expensive deal at the time. That move still seemed a long way off for me during those final few months at the Vetch.

CHAPTER 8

ENTER THE DRAGONS

*'The Battle of Wrexham was the dirtiest game of football I was
ever involved in, even if I didn't manage to stay on the pitch.'*
MEL CHARLES

WINNING INTERNATIONAL RECOGNITION is every
lad's dream and I was so proud when my day arrived, when I
could pull on the red shirt and dragon badge of Wales.
Although I had played for Swansea Schoolboys, I never did play
for Wales Schoolboys and whereas certain players came through
all the age groups, I was a latecomer in some respects to
international football.

I did play in the Wales Under-23 team, however, in a match
against England. They had Jimmy Greaves and Brian Clough in
their side. I was playing centre-half and I remember Cloughy had
a hell of a shot, although surprisingly he was pretty quiet back
then – the mouth hadn't fully developed at that stage. But despite
England having those two famous forwards in their side, not to

mention numerous other excellent players, we beat them 2-1 and that was a perfect introduction to international football for me and enough to give me a hunger for more. I was particularly chuffed after that game as I had been the captain; I wore the armband at Swansea Town too, and Haverfordwest and Porthmadog, but for me, most of the time wearing the armband didn't mean too much. Being captain of your country is a different matter of course, but for me being captain at club level was no big deal, you had leaders all over the pitch anyway – if you were captain it just meant that you tossed a bloody coin at the start of the match!

But playing for Wales meant everything to me. I remember how you used to learn that you had been picked. Although we had a team manager, the side would be picked by a committee of selectors. The first you heard whether you were in or out was when you listened to the radio, usually during the nine o' clock news on a Monday or Tuesday morning. I was a selfish bugger when it came to listening to the team. They would start going through the players in order: 'Kelsey, Hopkins…' and so on, and I think I only listened till they got to 'Number 4, Mel Charles', and then that was me happy, I wasn't bothered about the rest of them.

I was first capped by my country on 20 April 1955 against Northern Ireland in a match at Windsor Park, Belfast. There were two sets of brothers in the Wales team that day: myself and John, and Ivor and Lenny Allchurch. Together we posed for the cameras before the game. It was a massive game for me, my first senior international for my country, but it was also to prove a momentous occasion for John too – because he scored all three goals in a 3-2 win. Wales had also won 3-2 there on their last visit to Belfast in 1953, with John getting two, so he was chuffed to go one better this time.

Perhaps it was just because he wanted to impress his little brother, but whatever it was, John played out of his skin in that game at Windsor Park – he was outstanding. He got two goals in the first 17 minutes, before Ireland got it back to 2–2 before half-time, but then he came out for the second half and wrapped up his hat-trick with what turned out to be the winning goal, just four minutes after the restart. It's fair to say he overshadowed the young debutant that night and it was the first time I had lined up alongside him in the same team in a proper game. When I saw what he could do with my own eyes, I was impressed with the big fellow. The papers summed up his brilliant performance against the Irish the next day, with the *South Wales Evening Post* saying: 'Perhaps it would be better to put it this way – Charles 3, Ireland 2. For it was the Leeds centre forward who looked the only player of class.' Okay, I admit it, I had a quiet game. But although John scored a hat-trick in that game, I would go one better for Wales later in my career, something I never tired of ribbing him about.

I had made the breakthrough, and my chest was puffed out with pride at finally becoming a full Wales international, which was a dream come true. I would go on to represent my country at full international level another 30 times, and while I am now proud of my record of 31 appearances, back then I never did count my caps. You didn't get handed a cap after each individual match; the Welsh FA would present you with one cap a year with the initials of the countries you had played against embroidered on the peak. It was very different in those days though, and there could be years when you only played three or four internationals. Nowadays they have friendlies all the time and it seems that they find any excuse for an international, allowing some players to quickly notch up vast numbers of international appearances. But back in the Fifties international football was mainly confined to World Cup qualifiers and the odd Home International, with an end-of-season tour thrown in every now and again.

My second game in a Wales shirt is another one that I remember well, although it has gone down in history as an infamous match and most people will probably remember it simply as the 'Battle of Wrexham'.

We played against Austria at the Racecourse Ground on 23 November 1955, and it was meant to be a 'friendly', but it ended up being anything but. There had been a lot of bad blood simmering from a meeting between the two countries in Vienna, and it all spilled over 18 months later in north Wales, when the return game degenerated into a dreadful kicking match. That game also goes down in history as the only time I saw John really lose his temper on the football field.

Austria were a pretty useful side and had done very well at the World Cup the year before. They were strong and quick, proving themselves a real handful in Wrexham, and it wasn't long before we found ourselves two goals behind. Good as they were, they were also very, very dirty. They had taken great offence when Derek Tapscott and Trevor Ford started charging their goalkeeper, which it was legal to do back then. The French referee, quite rightly, didn't take any action against Tappy or Trevor, but that tipped the excitable Austrians over the edge and they started trying to dish out their own justice, with a lot of off-the-ball incidents and wild tackles setting the tone for the rest of the match.

With about 15 minutes to go, I had the ball out near the wing and two of their players started taking it in turns to try and chop me down. Just as I thought I had shielded the ball and shaken off their unwanted attentions, I took a hell of a kick from one of them. He just stuck the boot into me from behind, hard as he could, and it was enough to take me out of the game. I couldn't even stand up and had to be stretchered off. But while I was lying there crumpled in agony on the turf, John went tearing away after the guy who had done it, grabbed him by the jersey and lifted him off the ground. He screamed at him: 'If you ever do that to my brother again I'll bloody kill you!'

I had never seen him lose his temper in a match, and I don't think he ever did again, but it took a while for the whole team to calm him down. It was a remarkable sight, watching him lose his composure, but he only did it for me in that game. He was never booked in his career, of course – hence the 'Gentle Giant' nickname – but neither was I. Good as gold, us Charles boys!

We ended up losing the Battle of Wrexham 2-1, with Tappy getting our goal, but it's still a game that sends a shudder down the spine. It has also generated a lot of debate in the years since as to just how dirty it actually was, but I would like to set the record straight – it was bordering on a bloodbath!

For example, the match report in the *South Wales Evening Post* the next day tried to play it all down, claiming that it had just been a little bit rough but no harm done. Under the headline INTERNATIONAL TOUGH BUT NO BATTLE, their reporter Pat Searle wrote: 'Was this international as dirty as some make out? I watched the full 90 minutes and while conceding there were fouls by both sides, the scene never resembled a battlefield.' I would have to say that it is utter garbage – it was all very well him sitting in the press box making his judgment, but he wasn't on the end of a size 10 Austrian boot to the back of the leg! Maybe he would have been better suited as their rugby correspondent instead, because he added: 'Wales started the trouble and Austria retaliated with a vengeance. Down went the

Welshmen like ninepins – a quick sponge and up they jumped, all except Mel Charles, who went down and stayed there. Ligament trouble was diagnosed and Swansea Town will be short of his services for quite a while. Big brother John got a bumping, but all the offender got was a wagging finger from Charles himself – if only all soccer players were as cool and sporting.'

John may have been tremendously cool and sporting throughout his career, but he was far from it that night and I admired him for the fact he was ready to jump in for his brother. He certainly did a lot more than wag his finger when he saw me getting hacked down: he was pushed over the edge by the sight of his little brother taking a kicking, and he leapt to my defence, the same way he had done now and again when we were kids. Even as fully-grown men, he was there to look out for me.

Most people described the game exactly like it was – a bitterly unpleasant kicking match – and that's why the 'Battle of Wrexham' name was coined. The Austria coach said the match had 'degenerated into a game of rugby' and laid the blame on Wales, while the *Western Mail* newspaper called it a 'disgrace to national football'. Everybody rushed to have their say, and one of the greatest Austrian players of all time, Ernst Ocwirk, said: 'It was more like a boxing match than football.' So there you have it: it's safe to say that the Battle of Wrexham was indeed a battle and anyone who tells you otherwise is talking rubbish. For me, it was the dirtiest game of football I was ever involved in, even if I didn't manage to stay on the pitch for the full 90 minutes, thanks to my Austrian markers.

Despite the pain I suffered against Austria, I must have done okay in Belfast and in the Battle of Wrexham, because when the home international series started again in 1956, the selectors picked me and I became a regular fixture in the side, playing against England and Scotland that year. We drew 2-2 against Scotland at Ninian Park in October, Terry Medwin and Trevor Ford scoring the goals, but the England game the following month was something else. My first taste of Wembley was an experience I will never forget, as we found ourselves involved in one hell of a game.

Wales had started to develop a horrible habit of suffering bad luck against the English, who had some great players in their side. They had guys like Billy Wright playing, the great Stanley Matthews – who would later become a good friend of John and I – Tom Finney and Johnny Haynes. It was probably the best team England had had in a hell of a time. There was more than one occasion when we should have beaten them and didn't, and this was one of those days.

Our problems at Wembley began after just 15 minutes when our goalkeeper Jack Kelsey threw himself at the feet of Tom Finney, suffering a bad injury to his side. There were no substitutes allowed in those days, and for Jack to try and continue in goal would have been suicide: they would have just rained goals past him because he could barely move his arms. The only thing for it was to play him outfield, but he could only limp about and was more or less a passenger. I remember coming close myself with a shot from 40 yards, I couldn't have hit it better and was just about to start celebrating when somehow their goalkeeper Ted Ditchburn got a hand to it and kept it out. Because Wembley was such a big pitch, it was hard enough with eleven against eleven, so for Jack to suffer his injury was a nightmare and it meant the odds were stacking up against us. It was bad enough with Jack being injured, but then it was my turn to get crocked. Just before half-time, I took a really sore one on the thigh, and I was left hobbling about the pitch. We fought the best we could, to all intents and purposes with nine men, and eventually lost the game, but the mainly English crowd was going wild in appreciation of our efforts. Again, the *South Wales Evening Post* summed it up: 'If ever a case for substitutes was proved to the hilt it was in the England–Wales international at Wembley Stadium… where Wales were eventually beaten 3-1 after a positively heroic struggle against terrific odds. The 90,000 crowd roared its applause of a truly magnificent fight by the Welshmen, who by a strange coincidence experienced identically the same misfortune two years ago, only on that occasion Daniel and Sullivan were the casualties. John Charles was not quite at his best, but the disruption of his side prevented him from reaching those heights of brilliance crowds have come to expect. Nevertheless, his influence on brother Mel proved the selectors right, for the Swansea Town player turned in his best display for some time.'

It must have been some first half that I had, because all I can remember of the second half was shuffling about the Wembley pitch in blinding pain.

The final game of the 1956/57 home internationals saw me return to the scene of my first cap – Windsor Park – and while our 0-0 draw with Northern Ireland was not much to shout about it proved to be a significant match in more ways than one for John. It was after this game that he sealed his ground-breaking move to Juventus.

Juve's chief scout had approached him a few days before the game and told him they were interested in taking him over to Serie A from Leeds. And when we played in Belfast, their president was there to see John in action for Wales – not only that, he was captaining Wales for the first time. Real Madrid were supposed to be interested too, and Leeds were making noises that they wouldn't sell him to another English club, so it looked like a straight fight between the Spanish and Italian giants. Little more than a week after the draw in Ireland, Leeds conceded defeat and accepted an offer – John was going to Italy and was well on his way to superstardom.

I enjoyed all the internationals I played in, but the home internationals had a lot of extra excitement because you were coming up against a lot of the players that you were locking horns with in the Football League. The games against Scotland were always tough, they had some real hard defenders like big George Young of Rangers and they were a passionate team that played for the jersey like Wales. They had my mate Jackie Henderson in their team, who I got to know well when we were at Arsenal together. Although he was a Glaswegian, he played all of his football down in England, after joining Portsmouth straight from his National Service. We were good buddies at Arsenal together and he was a regular in the forward line at Highbury.

I remember one game up in Glasgow when the locals were swept away by John Charles fever. John was meeting up with us separately, coming straight from Italy, while we travelled up as a team. When we got to Central Station in Glasgow we noticed a big mass of people crowded round somebody at the end of the platform. We thought maybe there was a film star in town, but the closer we got and the more we heard people getting excited, we realised that the mega star in town was big John. They were mobbing him and pushing and shoving each other for a glimpse of the football superstar. And, of course, John was towering above them, modestly shaking hands and chatting away. He was already well used to that kind of adulation in Italy, and modest as he was, he took it all in his stride. Anyway, by the time we strode up alongside him in our Welsh blazers, nobody batted an eyelid. It was big John that they wanted to see; as far as they were concerned we were all bit-part players.

The atmosphere at Hampden was something else. It was a real cavern of a stadium and it was absolutely rammed full of loud Scots. When they talk about the Hampden Roar, it had to be heard to be believed. But the funny thing about the Scotland team was that while they were big and powerful at the back, their forward line always seemed to be made up of midgets. They were like a row of pygmies, but they had a really good team in those days and we didn't seem to get the better of them for a long while.

The games against England were the most enjoyable for us, though. If you can't get yourself motivated as a Welshman for a game against the English, then you're not a Welshman. The only problem in that era was that they had a fantastic side and they were incredibly difficult to play against. As I said before, there was more than one time when we should have beaten them and another game that we probably should have won was the fixture up at Villa Park in 1958.

It was unusual for an international to be staged at Villa Park and after the night we played there, England didn't return to play another match there for 43 years. But we left Birmingham having put on a show. I was marking Nat Lofthouse in that game, and he never got a kick. The next night Juventus were playing a challenge match at Highbury, so John had to go straight from Villa Park to play in that game. There was no messing about in those days; you could play two games in two days some times, and you wouldn't complain about it, either. We really should have beaten England comfortably at Villa Park and led twice, thanks to goals from Ivor Allchurch and Derek Tapscott, but Peter Broadbent equalised twice and somehow they wriggled off the hook. Once again an injury to a key man was to cost us dear, this time Dave Bowen being the unfortunate victim. He took a bad one to his shoulder early on, and there wasn't much that he could do but hobble around the pitch in pain. Our heroic efforts, basically playing with ten men against a strong English team, were not lost on Bill Paton of the *South Wales Evening Post*, who gave us a lot of credit in his match report. The headline in the paper was: 'A mighty epic fight by Wales' and he wrote: 'Welsh soccer prestige rocketed sky-high at Villa Park, where after twice taking the lead Wales had to be content with a draw against the might of England. The record books will record a 2-2 draw, but morally, at any rate, the honours went to 11 gallant Welshmen. Ten to be exact, for skipper Dave Bowen sustained a shoulder injury before half time that made him virtually a passenger. The Welsh defence carried a more solid and compact look, with Mel Charles having what I considered to be one of his best internationals. What a grand fighter the Swansea skipper is when the odds are biggest. He had the measure of Lofthouse throughout and, showing keen anticipation, relentlessly broke up the English attacks before they had a chance to blossom.' It was certainly one of my best games for Wales and I don't think Nat Lofthouse played for England again after that match.

CHAPTER 9

SWEDE DREAMS

'I knew nothing really about the World Cup − I'd just heard the odd snippet every now and again, and never thought I'd actually play in one.'
MEL CHARLES

THE WORLD CUP WASN'T REALLY a competition we were familiar with − it didn't enjoy the massive profile it does now − but we were determined to give it our best shot in trying to qualify for the finals in Sweden in 1958. But when the draw for qualifying was made we landed in a very tough section, paired with East Germany and Czechoslovakia in Group Four.

Not long after John's transfer to Juventus had gone through, we started our campaign in promising style with a 1-0 win over the Czechs at Ninian Park, a match in which Colin Webster won his first cap for Wales. All eyes were on John though. It was something of a farewell to Britain for him, and everyone wanted to see him do well to show that the price Juve had paid for him had been money well spent. Juventus also had a posse of officials in the stand, praying that nothing happened to their big-money buy and that they were able to get him to Italy safely and in one piece. He didn't disappoint the crowd, or his new club, and he and Jack Kelsey were outstanding to give us two points and put us seemingly in a good position to qualify. It had been a close-run thing though, and we were far from our best in that game. A late goal from Roy Vernon gave us two points we scarcely deserved, and we had a lot of reasons to be thankful to John and Jack Kelsey. The crowd went ballistic at the end of the game, rushing on the pitch to give John a pat on the back and wish him well for his new life in Italy, and it needed the coppers to come on and make a path for him to get from the pitch to the dressing room.

Winning your home games in a World Cup qualifying series is a must, but you also have to pick up a result or two in the away matches, and Wales had a habit of going to pieces whenever we played on the continent. So when we travelled to face East Germany and Czechoslovakia in a double-header we knew we would have to produce something special if we were to stay in pole position in the group.

First up was East Germany and it was a culture shock for us. Leipzig was in a hell of a state. We stayed at the Astoria hotel, and it was nice enough, but as soon as you ventured outside the confines of the building you realised you were in a bleak place. It was a communist regime, where everything seemed to be controlled. I don't know if it was just us being paranoid, but it seemed that there were blokes wearing white macs everywhere you went, watching you. They were probably watching us more closely as we had come from the West, but it was all a bit unsettling and it wasn't easy to relax.

True to Wales' woeful away form we lost the game, and I even managed to upset big John before a ball was kicked. Because I was superstitious, I always tried to make sure I ran out last when the team came out of the tunnel. As I ran out from the tunnel at the big concrete Zentralstadion, someone stopped me and handed me this big bouquet of flowers. I just said thanks very much, and grabbed them and continued on my way out on to the pitch, where the teams were starting to line up in front of the main stand for the national anthems. But it turned out that whoever was in charge of handing out the flowers had mistaken me for John, and because they had managed to miss him coming out, they took one look at me and thought I must be him. I did look like him after all, so it was an easy enough mistake to make. I was also about to make a big mistake myself because I had no idea that the flowers had been meant for John, and that it was a tradition for the captain of the team to hand them over at the start. I turned to Dave Bowen, who was standing next to me in the line for the national anthems, and asked him what I was meant to do with them. He didn't have the foggiest either so he said: 'I dunno, Mel, just chuck them into the crowd'. So that's what I did, I just ran over to the stand and tossed them in and the crowd went wild. There was a massive crowd at the game, over 100,000, and the noise was deafening.

Just as I was feeling quite pleased with myself at doing my bit for Welsh–German relations, I saw John coming over towards me absolutely raging – he was effing and blinding and calling me a stupid so and so. He said he'd spent the last five minutes looking for those bloody flowers. I don't think big John was too impressed when I said that at least I'd won us a bit of backing from the crowd by throwing the flowers to them. But the crowd could have given us all the backing in the world, and it still wouldn't have done us any good. The annoying thing was that we got off to a blinding start. I scored after six minutes and that was enough for John to forgive me the flowers incident, but the East Germans were a strong side; they were swarming all over us and fully deserved their 2-1 victory.

That win opened the group up, and if we were to stay in the hunt for a place at the finals we really needed a win a week later in Prague. But we had big problems with injuries as Dave Bowen and Derek Tapscott both picked up knocks against the Germans. We had only travelled out to Eastern Europe with the bare minimum of players and we had to send for Des Palmer and Ray Daniel to join us in Prague, otherwise we wouldn't even have been able to field a team. That was the way the Welsh FA did things then. Instead of taking a couple of extra players to cover for injuries, they would stick a committee man on the plane instead. It was madness.

We flew on from Germany to Czechoslovakia in a little plane and stayed at the Hotel Paris. Like Leipzig, the place in general was a bit down in the dumps and life behind the Iron Curtain looked grim, with little money around, and while the people were always very friendly, there was no mistaking that they were a bit twitchy too. It was a beautiful city to look at though, but you just didn't know what went on behind the scenes in those places and it was obvious that the folk there were enduring a very different way of life to the one we were living back in Swansea.

The Czech team, who had given us a severe test in the opening match in Cardiff, were even better on their own patch, and again we couldn't have any complaints about losing the game, this time 2-0, although I had a decent game myself in Dukla Prague's ground, the Stadion Juliska. The Welsh journalists who had come along for the trip sent some gloomy words back to the homeland about our prospects of qualifying for the finals. The *Evening Post* informed its readers: 'The long-distance impression may be one of a bitter struggle waged between two teams of near to equal merit. Not on your life! Swallow the bitter pill. Mel Charles was excellent, but the Czechs were so fast, so persistent and so elusive that even five men ringing the Welsh goal could not keep them at bay for long. Kelsey had a giant's job; his goal was busier than Piccadilly Circus on Cup final night.'

That defeat killed off our chances because Czechoslovakia had beaten East Germany twice and were assured of top spot in the group. In that World Cup qualifying series we won our home games in Cardiff, but a bit like at club level, with Swansea, our away form wasn't up to scratch and it seemed like we had missed out. It looked all set to be the kind of glorious failure that has dogged Wales for these last 50 years.

There were also worrying reports that Juventus were determined to stop John playing for Wales, and while they had grudgingly allowed him to go along on the trip to Eastern Europe for the two World Cup games, the word on the street was that they wouldn't be so generous in the future. To begin with, Juventus were actually pretty decent when it came to releasing John. Of course, there were a few occasions when they put their foot down and said he couldn't come along, but most of the time they allowed him to join up with the Wales squad for internationals, probably to keep him sweet as he quickly developed into their star player and there was practically nothing they wouldn't do to make sure he was 100 per cent happy. Still, the statistics don't lie, and in his five years in Turin, John took part in only 14 games for Wales.

In this particular case John wasn't given permission to complete the World Cup qualifying series. We thought he would be allowed to come to Cardiff, but maybe because our chance of making the finals had gone, Juventus had a change of heart and said he couldn't play. Our last game of the three-team qualifying group was the home match against East Germany, which was played on 25 September 1957 in Cardiff, and while I gave one of my best performances in a Welsh shirt and managed to score at both ends in a 4–1 win, we were still to miss out on an automatic place at the finals.

Our manager Jimmy Murphy was a great motivator and was able to fire us up rather than relying on tactics, and that was definitely the case before the match in Cardiff. He was probably still smarting from our defeat in Leipzig and before we played East Germany in the return match, he gave a stirring team talk, even if it would not exactly be judged politically correct now. He said: 'Lads, you know these bastards you are playing today, East Germany; don't forget they bombed your mothers and fathers.' He never said another word and just walked out the dressing room and left us there with our thoughts. It had the desired effect and we played well, with me at centre-half and Graham Vearncombe making his debut in goal in place of Jack Kelsey, who was unavailable that night.

Those fickle reporters in the press, who had been slating us five months earlier after our defeat in Czechoslovakia, gushed with praise the next day. The *Evening Post* gave the headline to me, saying: 'Mel Gives His Answer – shines at centre-half for Wales.' The report explained: 'Swansea Town supporters, who have long felt that Mel Charles is the man to fill the club's problem spot, received more than adequate confirmation at Ninian Park, Cardiff, when he fully justified the Welsh selectors' confidence in him at centre-half during Wales 4–1 win over East Germany. Only once did Mel put a foot wrong. Unfortunately it was the foot which scored East Germany's goal. But this apart, he competently and capably blotted out the middle, refusing to be led a-wandering by will o' the wisp centre forward Willi Troger.' Troger was some player right enough. One of the best and trickiest forwards I played against, he had lost his right hand during the war, but this didn't seem to affect his balance in any way and you had to concentrate 100 per cent to keep tabs on him and mark him closely.

Although it was a bittersweet moment to win so convincingly yet still walk off the pitch thinking you'd blown your chance of playing in the World Cup finals, it was nice to get a good performance under my belt. It was also good to see Des Palmer, a talented centre-forward with Swansea Town, getting a hat-trick as well. Maybe my performance at centre-half in that match also made up Jimmy Murphy's mind where he was going to play me in the bigger matches that we would face in the future.

I didn't do quite so well in my next match in the centre of defence though, I have to admit. In fact, none of the Wales team did very well, and we found ourselves on the wrong end of a 4-0 thumping at the hands of England. It was an embarrassing match for us that started badly and got worse. Mel Hopkins scored an own goal after just a few minutes, and I think we were suffering from some kind of hangover at not making it through our World Cup group. Johnny Haynes also scored in the first half and by half-time Jimmy Murphy was raging. He got stuck into us in the dressing room as any good Welshman would do when you're losing face to England in your own backyard. He was telling us to show a bit more fight and to start getting stuck into them, and when one of the boys took issue with that and said 'Come on, we're giving them some stick', Jimmy quickly shut him up by saying: 'Giving them some stick, are we? Well, you tell me why they keep getting up!' He was good at the one-liners, Jimmy. Not always a man for big long speeches, but he was great at getting his point across when he had to.

We headed towards 1958 still hurting at coming close, but not close enough to secure a place at the World Cup through our group games, but then something beyond our wildest dreams happened – we were about to be handed a very lucky second chance to join England, Scotland and Northern Ireland at the biggest tournament of them all.

Politics in the Middle East gave us an unexpected lifeline, and because the Arab and Asian countries were refusing to play Israel, they needed another team to face them in a play-off for the last spot in the finals. A draw at FIFA's headquarters in Switzerland saw us selected from a pot full of lucky losers to face Israel in a two-leg play-off, with a place at the finals in Sweden up for grabs. We had literally won the lottery! In fact, I think Uruguay had been plucked out of the hat first, but they refused because they reckoned it would hurt their pride to accept charity. Wales weren't going to pass up such a glorious opportunity though, no way! The news came over on the wireless and we celebrated our good fortune.

I must say I knew nothing about the World Cup, really – I'd just heard the odd little story about it every now and again, and never thought I'd actually play in one. All through the group games against East Germany and the Czechs I clung to the dream that I might actually play in one, and while it was disappointing when we finished second behind the Czechs, I had just resigned myself to trying again for the 1962 finals instead. So when this second chance came up, everyone was buzzing with excitement and we were absolutely determined not to let such a glorious opportunity pass through our fingers. We didn't know anything about Israel either, but from what we heard they were largely an amateur outfit, and if we were going to make a mess of things, it would not be through fear of playing them. Without being cocky, we fancied our chances.

The first match, on 15 January 1958, was to be played in Israel with the return leg back in Cardiff three weeks later. Israel was a beautiful place, but flying into Tel Aviv you could see all the sheds and shacks on the left-hand side as we came in to land. I thought it would be a country full of millionaires, but as you were going in, it was a real eye-opener. We weren't exactly coming from the richest of countries and money was tight in Wales, but this was real poverty in the raw. There was more good news for us when we learned that Juventus had decided to let John play in both games, and although he had a chaperone with him from the club, fussing over him everywhere he went, it was great to have him with us. You could see even then that life was treating him well in Italy, and his sun-tan stood out among the rest of us, who had been freezing away all winter in Cardiff, Swansea and all over England. They held a dinner in our honour and I remember cringing when John got up and started singing the song 'That Old Black Magic' – not the best choice when a lot of folk there were coloured. But it was perfectly innocent, and no one batted an eyelid, it was the superstar John Charles after all and he could do no wrong!

When we got to the ground, the Ramat Gan Stadium, it was only half-built and more or less still under construction – it was like playing on a building site. It was very hot too, and not easy to get used to, having come from the depths of winter in Britain. The Israelis were very hospitable folk though, and when they came to Wales for the return leg, their Football Association sent every player crates of oranges as a goodwill gesture. They sent them round in a case to my house – I didn't know what to do with them all, and ended up selling them round the pubs – quite a few drinkers in Swansea got their share of Vitamin C on the back of that!

We had plenty of confidence that we would beat Israel because they were not a top-class team and sure enough, we beat them 2-0 there through goals from Ivor Allchurch and Dave Bowen, then 2-0 again in Cardiff, Ivor again getting one and Cliffy getting the other. The return was played on a cold, wet winter's night and there were 50,000 crammed into Ninian Park, so any lingering hopes they had of turning it round were quickly washed away. The match in Cardiff was notable for the heroics of their goalkeeper Yaakov Chodorov, who became something of a legend in his homeland, and they reckon the performance he turned in that night was the best ever by an Israeli international. Only problem was, he finished the game in hospital with a broken nose – courtesy of John! He'd already made save after save and when the two of them went up for a high ball near the end there was an almighty crack and he was pole-axed – a complete accident, but that was the end of the game for him and I think he got quite an ovation as he was stretchered off. The Israel team had to fly ahead and leave him in hospital in Cardiff as he had concussion and wasn't fit to go anywhere. But John was the first to visit him in hospital, and quite a few of the Welsh team popped in to see him and some lasting friendships were formed. In fact, he stayed in touch with Jack Kelsey, and would still go and see Arsenal games at Highbury from time to time when Jack took to running the souvenir shop when his playing days came to an end.

While the Israel team prepared to go home, we celebrated our World Cup qualification with a few beers in the Park Hotel. But the same night of that game the face of British football was to change forever when the Busby Babes' plane crashed in Munich, killing 23 of the 43 passengers on board. Jimmy Murphy would have been on that plane, had he not been taking us for the match against Israel and the crash, and its aftermath, cast a dark shadow over him. He had to take the team while Matt Busby was recovering in hospital and he had a lot of emotional trauma to deal with. His contribution to Manchester United during those dark days and the role he played in rebuilding them alongside Busby should never be underestimated.

Another lad from Swansea, a winger Kenny Morgans, who would almost certainly have come with us to the World Cup, had been on the plane in Munich. Although he was one of the survivors of the crash, his career was never quite the same. Eventually he went back to Swansea Town after a couple more years at Manchester United. Colin Webster was another Busby Babe, but he missed the crash as he was in his bed with flu. He had another five or six years at Old Trafford before he too came back to Swansea Town; he was a great character. Another future Swan who was on the plane that fateful night was Harry Gregg, the brilliant Northern Irish international keeper, who proved a hero by helping pull people from the wreckage. He still made it to the World Cup in Sweden that summer, proving himself to be one of the best goalkeepers in the world, and he would play a part in the Swansea story a few years later – joining the club in the late Sixties and then going on to become manager after they graduated from being Swansea Town to Swansea City, as we know them today.

Gregg's life would be haunted by the memories of Munich though and it was a terrible time for Jimmy Murphy too; it would deeply affect him until his dying day. For him, the only ray of light was that he would have the honour of leading Wales to the World Cup finals. Against all the odds we were heading to Sweden and the biggest stage of our careers.

CHAPTER 10

MEXICANS, MAGYARS AND MAYHEM

'Jimmy Murphy has done it again! The man who stepped in after the Munich air disaster to rebuild the shattered remnants of Manchester United has now piloted Wales – "the country without a chance" – to the quarter-finals of the World Cup at their first attempt.'
South Wales Evening Post

WE THOUGHT THE SQUAD that had beaten Israel would be more or less the same one that we took to Sweden, but nevertheless it still gave you goosebumps to hear your name read out on the wireless as part of the official squad. I just couldn't relax until I heard the clipped tones of the radio announcer saying 'Mel Charles' and only when I heard my name read out did I finally believe that I was part of that elite group who would be making the trip to the World Cup finals.

I wasn't particularly nervous beforehand but the butterflies had started with a vengeance by the time I got there. Mind you, it wasn't exactly the smoothest of preparations for the finals. There was another monumental mix-up before we even flew out from London, courtesy of the bungling powers-that-be at the Welsh Football Association. Somehow, the committee hadn't managed to book any formal training facilities for us and instead of being put through our paces at one of the London stadiums or training grounds, we had to train instead in Hyde Park. Can you imagine it, a team of international footballers warming up for the World Cup in a public park! But the main problem with Hyde Park was that there were no ball games allowed, so when we threw down the tracksuits for goalposts and started having a kick-about, the park-keeper came flying over, screaming blue murder at us, and threw us off. We were all trying to be as professional as we could and were focusing on the job that would await us over in Scandinavia, but instead we were running around daft among the pigeons, ponds and angry parkies in a London park.

We had five days in London at our unusual training camp, and then got on a flight to Bromma airport on 2 June. Again there were rumblings that the Italians were not going to play ball and let John come and join us. Juventus had originally given their word that he would be released without any interference, but the Italian FA had thrown a spanner in the works and threatened to stop him playing in Sweden. Naturally the selectors and Jimmy Murphy were getting very nervous as our first game approached, as a lot of the plans and expectations were centred on John being allowed to play. As our first match crept closer and closer, they still didn't have any official word if he would be joining us or not. We had a big enough squad with us, but the thought of being deprived of our best player was unsettling for everyone. Really, there was no option but to sit tight and hope that all the red-tape would be unravelled in time for him to take part.

It was very warm in Sweden and we quickly settled into our base for the tournament in Soltsjobaden – a beautiful place, a little island right in the middle of a cluster of lakes, just outside Stockholm. The host country, Sweden, were in our group along with Hungary and Mexico, and the Swedes were wonderful towards us as we settled in.

If we thought we had been given a warm welcome by the locals, the biggest welcome of all was reserved for the one missing member of the party – John – who had finally received clearance to play in the World Cup and was on his way. I remember we were all sitting in this big room having a meal, two days before our first game against Hungary, when John walked in and the Welsh FA directors and their wives threw down their knives and forks, got to their feet and started clapping and singing 'For he's a jolly good fellow' – what a bunch of prats! I have never seen anything like it and John went crimson with embarrassment. We were happy to see him too, mind you, but we stopped short of making an exhibition of ourselves like they did.

There was a definite gulf between the players and the committee members. It was hard to respect them when a lot of the time it looked like they were more interested in the perks that came with these trips than the actual football or the players that had got them there. It didn't pay to rock the boat with them, though, because at the end of the day they were the ones who picked the team and if you had a fall-out with them then you could kiss goodbye to your international career because they had the clout to leave you out in the cold if you made an enemy out of them.

Occasionally their amateurism left me astounded. When we went to Sweden the selectors had only booked flights to stay for one week, when the group matches ended, because they didn't expect us to last out there. Talk about pessimism! But when we made it through to the quarter-finals they had to pay for their lack of faith and were left red-faced because they then had to first fly back to London and then back to Sweden in time for the quarter-finals. One or two of them really seemed to know nothing about football at all. There was no rapport between the players and officials, and it was often a 'them and us' attitude with two distinct camps. There wasn't much mingling and we were happier to mix with the boys from the press than make small-talk with the men in suits. Mind you, we looked the part out there. We had all been kitted out for the finals at a tailor in London and were given these smart black blazers to wear. But despite looking like the office-bearers accompanying us on the trip, in terms of what we were wearing, that was where the similarity ended. It wasn't a case of us being difficult, it was just that we had absolutely nothing in common and some of them didn't even seem to know anything about football. They were just in it for the trips and the prestige, I think, and it was a bit of a class divide.

With John safely cleared to play for us, he was the final piece of the jigsaw in our preparations. This also allowed Jimmy Murphy to put his plan for the Charles brothers into action – I would be playing centre-half at the World Cup and John would be centre-forward. A lot of emphasis would be put on our physical strength and our ability to defend because Jimmy was adamant that we would not just be making up the numbers at the World Cup, nor were we going to embarrass ourselves in any way. If that meant defending first, then so be it, but we would be nobody's fools.

While at least 90 per cent of the attention from the press, locals and opposition players and coaches seemed to focus on John, who by that time was already a worldwide star, we had lots of other good players in our squad too and all the limelight on John probably helped us to surprise a lot of people. When everybody was fit, Wales were able to field a great team in Sweden. In goal was Jack Kelsey: a real master of arts, he was the governor at the time, probably the best goalkeeper in Britain and one of the finest in the world. Stuart Williams was the right-back, barrel-chested and dependable. Left-back was Mel Hopkins, who was a big mate of mine. Then you had Derek Sullivan, who played for Cardiff. We were all working-class but he was *real* working-class; he'd fought his way up the hard way and was hard as nails on the pitch. Dave Bowen was a great player and a fantastic leader, really good at lifting those around him whenever the chips were down. We had Terry Medwin on the wing; Ron Hewitt, Colin Webster, Ivor Allchurch, Cliffy Jones, the list goes on – like I say, we were a great team when we were all fit.

After all the training and waiting around we were desperate to get started and we kicked off Wales' first-ever World Cup finals campaign with a 1-1 draw against Hungary. It was in a stadium known as the Iron Ground in a place called Sandviken, where the Hungarians were based for the tournament, which gave them a bit of an advantage, I suppose, as we had to go on a fairly lengthy bus ride before the game to get there. Hungary had been finalists at the 1954 World Cup, eventually losing to West Germany, but their country was in political turmoil by 1958 and there had been a big uprising shortly before the finals. This basically meant that the team that came to Sweden was virtually unrecognisable from the one that had gone so close to winning the tournament four years earlier. Ferenc Puskas and a few of the other 'Magical Magyars' were long gone and it soon become clear early in the game that the eleven guys we were facing were nothing out of the ordinary. They were still known as the Magyars, but I think they were clinging to past glories a little. Without Puskas and Co, their magic had ebbed away.

Wearing canary yellow for the night, we were still the underdogs, as World Cup unknowns, and when Hungary took the lead with a goal from Josef Bozsik, one of the few survivors from their 1954 side, I'm sure most of the neutrals in the crowd were starting to think that we were simply in the tournament to make up the numbers. Little Wales were all set to live up to the pessimists' view that by sneaking in the back door to the finals, we were certain to be the World Cup whipping boys. They hadn't reckoned on the Welsh fighting spirit though, and John soon showed how important he was to our campaign when he equalised for us by heading in a corner from a Cliffy Jones cross ten minutes after we had gone behind. It was an absolute cracker of a header too. We were both good in the air, John and me, and although we were tall, a lot of it was in the timing too. But when we had the chance to use that gift to good effect in the box, we got a whole load of goals. That was a textbook header from John, he just outjumped them all and met it perfectly, and all of a sudden it was a case of 'game on'. We pushed hard for a winner, but couldn't find one. The *Evening Post* said 'Wales recovered from the blow of an early goal to give a white-hot exhibition of Celtic fury, which deserved to bring them victory'. Yes, we should have won that game, but when we got on the bus back to Soltsjobaden we could be fairly happy with a point and a solid start to the World Cup. You couldn't help but feel those butterflies before the first game that it might all go wrong and that you might embarrass yourself and lose all three games, but early in that game we settled into a good rhythm and we didn't look out of place. We had shown we were worthy of our place at the finals and we were looking forward to

Above: Football was in my genes and my father Ned was a highly successful amateur player with Cwm Athletic before a broken leg ended his career.

Below: John and me together in 1955. Always the gentleman and an enormous influence on my own career, I had nothing but pride in my big brother's achievements. We played against each other when he was at Leeds United and I was at Swansea Town.

© PA Photos

SWANSEA TOWN F.C. 1958

Left to right - Back row :- Lawson, Nurse, John, King, Kennedy, Hughes, Griffiths, Williams, W.Boyes (Trainer).
Front row :- L.Allchurch, Davies, M.Charles, Palmer, Webster.

Above: The proud captain of my home-town heroes Swansea Town, but the club was renowned for cashing on their prize assets and I was months away from being sold. My destination was Highbury.

Below: We were the talk of the town when Swansea hosted a triple wedding in 1958: Don Pearson, Jeff Rees and I all said 'I do' to our respective brides. Vera and I were joined by the other two happy couples on a honeymoon to London, before returning to training just a couple of days later – there wasn't a lot of time for romance in those days!

Above: We drew with group rivals Hungary in our first meeting at the 1958 World Cup finals in Sandviken, but we showed all our fighting qualities to beat them 2-1 in a play-off. Here, Terry Medwin and I tangle with the Hungarian centre forward Laszlo Budai.

Below: Trying to keep tabs on the boy wonder Pelé, then aged 17, in the quarter-finals. We matched Brazil almost every step of the way, but Pelé scored his first ever World Cup goal to break Welsh hearts. His shirt was mine to keep after the game, and it would later be worn by a few lucky players in the Swansea Sunday pub leagues.

MEL CHARLES (Swansea Town and Wales)

Above left: Happy days at our home in Southgate, London, during my time at Arsenal as Vera and I play with our new baby son, Jeremy. He would later follow in my footsteps and play for Swansea and Wales.

Above right: As Arsenal's record signing there was a lot of pressure on me, but knee injuries made it difficult for me to live up to the great expectations.

Below left: Injuries came thick and fast for me during my spell with Arsenal, but at least I had my faithful dog Twinkle for company as I put my feet up and recovered at home.

© *Evening News*

Below right: I always loved playing at Highbury and the Arsenal fans were fantastic towards me. Here I am in action against Nottingham Forest in September 1959.

© *PA Photos*

THE FOOTBALL ASSOCIATION OF WALES LTD

6D   OFFICIAL
PROGRAMME   6D

WALES v IRELAND

VETCH FIELD, SWANSEA
WEDNESDAY, 11th APRIL, 1962
Kick Off 7.15 p.m.

THE FOOTBALL ASSOCIATION

INTERNATIONAL MATCH

ENGLAND
v
WALES

Photo by A. Wilkes & Son, West Bromwich.

At VILLA PARK, BIRMINGHAM
WEDNESDAY, NOVEMBER 26th 1958
KICK - OFF 2-0 P.M.

Official Programme   -   -   *Sixpence*

EUROPEAN NATIONS CUP INTERNATIONAL MATCH

WALES v. HUNGARY

NINIAN PARK, CARDIFF
WEDNESDAY, 20th MARCH, 1963
Kick-off 7.15 p.m.

Official Programme   •   One Shilling

The matchday programmes from three international matches close to my heart: our clash with England at Villa Park in 1958, where I gave one of my best performances in a Wales shirt as we came agonisingly close to an historic victory; the game against Ireland in 1962, which was switched from the Vetch to Ninian Park, where I scored all four goals in arguably my greatest match; and the match against Hungary in 1963 which was to be the last of my 31 caps.

Above: I had some good times at Cardiff City and I scored the club's last goal in top-flight football before they were relegated.   *© Western Mail & Echo*

Below: I was treated like a king by the fans at Porthmadog – one of them even wrote a poem about me – and I enjoyed some of the best times of my football career there. We won more than our fair share of trophies and it gave me back my hunger for football. Here we are lining up for the 1966–67 season.

Above: I was tempted back into to the Football League from Porthmadog to sign for Port Vale, where I teamed up with Jackie Mudie (pictured) and the great Sir Stanley Matthews.

Below: I played nearly 200 games with Haverfordwest, the other 'Bluebirds' of Wales. It was a great place for us old-timers to wind down our careers. You might also notice a certain Golden Boy called Ivor Allchurch sitting next to me in this team photo from 1971–72 – that lad could play a bit!

Above: I am happily settled as a pensioner living back in Swansea now, living just yards from my beloved Vetch Field, and I still treasure all my football memories, with no regrets.
© *South Wales Evening Post*

Below: The surviving members of Wales's one and only appearance at the World Cup in 1958 take a bow on the 50th anniversary of the finals, during Wales's match against Georgia at the Liberty Stadium in Swansea.
© *Nick Potts/PA Wire/PA Photos*

proving this further in our remaining two group games against Sweden and Mexico.

Our next test was against Mexico, and because they had been turned over 3–0 by Sweden in their first match, a lot of people expected it to be a walk in the park for us, basing their assumption on the strength of our draw with the previously highly-rated Hungarians. In typical fashion, Jimmy Murphy had been slagging the Mexicans off before the game in his team-talk, telling us that they were 'rubbish and only good for riding horses' – maybe he had been watching too many Westerns. It wasn't so much that Jimmy wanted to be disrespectful to our opponents, it was just his way of trying to instil in us that we were better than them and had nothing at all to fear. He could shoot down anyone's reputation with a few well-chosen words, and took the opportunity whenever it presented itself.

Jimmy had Mexico watched against Sweden and was not impressed with what he heard. But the truth was they were a stuffy side and they were obviously hurting from losing their opening game and doubly determined to make sure that they didn't roll over so easily a second time. They too were driven by the fear of embarrassing themselves on the world's biggest stage. The game was in the Solna Stadium in Stockholm, and to be honest we should have won. I still can't pinpoint the reason why, but we just didn't click into gear in that match. Ivor Allchurch scored early and everyone watching simply assumed that we were going to run out comfortable winners the way Sweden had done. But after taking the lead, instead of relaxing, we couldn't string two passes together and we were all over the place. If we had won, we wouldn't have deserved it, and when Mexico equalised in the last minute none of us could argue that we had it coming.

We got slated in the press for our lacklustre display. Billy

McGowran, the *Evening Post*'s man in Sweden, gave credit to our opponents, saying: 'the soaring Mexican eagles flew so high and so fast that the leathery wings of the Red Dragon were flapping like distress signals at the end of this thrill-a-second World Cup tie. Although they looked more like the Welshmen we know in their own red shirts again, they were only a shadow of the daffodil-clad side which shook the Mighty Magyars.' Mervyn Thomas, who was there covering the tournament for the *South Wales Echo*, was far more critical though and he said: 'I have seen Wales play some bad internationals. This time they were so downright disappointing that few of them deserve one halfpenny of the £50 they each picked up for playing. In fact, I suggested to them that they should donate their fees to some worthy charity.' That was a nice sentiment, and there is no getting away from the fact that we were really bad in that match, but a drawn game at the World Cup was not enough to persuade me to part with any of the money I had been paid, worthy charity or not!

The Mexican team had been decent though and it couldn't have been easy for them playing so far from home. They even had a handful of supporters out there too; I remember that because they came piling over the fence and chased Colin Webster off the field because he was giving them the old V-sign at the end. He could be a loose canon at times, but he was quite a character!

Two games down, two draws, and Wales were still unbeaten at the World Cup. Our chances of staying in the tournament hinged on our third group game, which was our meeting with the host nation, managed by Englishman George Raynor. But the game against Sweden also ended in a draw, goalless this time. They were a big physical team with a back line of strapping defenders. It maybe helped us that they had already qualified for the quarter-finals and that they had the luxury of being able to rest one or two players for their match against us. We knew that if we drew, we would be guaranteed at least a play-off and Jimmy set the team out that way. The way the other results had gone, with Sweden beating Hungary 2-1, then Hungary beating Mexico 4-0, we knew that our fate was in our own hands. Although the Hungarians had a better goal difference, we just needed a draw to end the group level with them on three points, and we weren't going to do anything rash and jeopardise our chances. A draw would do just nicely. Sweden seemed happy enough with that outcome too and during their match one or two of their players would sidle up alongside you and whisper: 'Drawn game, good result for us both'.

I don't think the fans were too happy, though, as both teams plodded their way to a 0-0 draw, with a few boos and whistles ringing around the ground as the sides played a cagey match with little incident to excite. But Jimmy Murphy's target for that game had been simply to keep us in the competition, and he succeeded. It was enough to keep us in with a chance of the quarter-finals, with a second game against Hungary two days later needed to decide who would join the Swedes in the last eight, and Jimmy wasn't going to apologise to anyone. 'I admit the game was not very exciting for the crowd, but it worked out as we had planned,' he told reporters afterwards. 'Our tactics were to make sure of not being beaten. The big thing is that we are still alive to fight another day. This time last week nobody gave us a dog's chance, but we have come through still unbeaten in spite of our limitations as one of the smallest countries. I am very proud of all of the boys, very proud indeed.'

We had already surpassed most people's pre-tournament expectations, and the *Evening Post* report reflected that: 'Wales are still in the World Cup. Tomorrow evening the Welsh team will meet the Hungarians in a play-off to decide which team from Group Three will accompany Sweden into the quarter-finals of the world's leading soccer tournament. Yes, little Wales, the side they said had no right to be in the competition, have done as well as England and better than Scotland.' The expectations of the Welsh FA officials had also been exposed. They had to hop on the plane back to London with their tails between their legs and then board another flight to rejoin us. We had a good laugh at that, and their embarrassed faces matched our red shirts.

The first Hungary game had been a bit rough, but it's safe to say the second one got a bit out of hand, with John assaulted every time he went near the ball, and plenty of times when he was nowhere near it. Because he had scored the goal in the first game and been a constant thorn in Hungary's side, he was a marked man second time around. We were in the same stadium as we had been for the Sweden game, but because it was a play-off, not many folk bothered to turn up. The atmosphere was a bit eerie, and the hardy souls that had paid to get in were witness to some nasty play from the Hungarians. The referee was on their side – he was Russian and I think it was an Iron Curtain thing, favouring them as fellow Eastern Europeans. He gave John no protection and turned a blind eye when we had a couple of penalty shouts, with John being chopped down in the box. They were kicking the hell out of him and getting away with it, and John, being the sportsman and gentleman that he was, never retaliated, which probably infuriated them more and made them even more determined to boot him off the pitch.

We had to show our professionalism in that game because we could have lost the plot when Hungary went ahead. It seemed everything was going against us, with a little help from the Russian ref. But then Ivor Allchurch scored an incredible goal, a left-foot volley from the edge of the box that flew like a missile into the top corner. They voted that into a top 50 Greatest World Cup goals on Channel Five recently, right up there with Maradona and Carlos Alberto. It was good seeing Ivor's goal in Sweden in there among the very best, and it deserves to be – I suppose with Wales it was all about quality rather than quantity, given that we only ever got to one World Cup. But for Ivor to score a spectacular goal was nothing new to me – I saw him do it time and time again in a Swansea shirt, and he was still doing it when we played alongside one another at Cardiff and later Haverfordwest County.

Ivor's goal against Hungary gave us renewed belief and although the bruised and battered John was limping around the pitch by that stage, with 15 minutes left we got the winner. Terry Medwin banged one in and while the brutal treatment John had received was enough to end his World Cup, our 2-1 win meant our adventure would continue – against tournament favourites Brazil. The press were lapping it up, no doubt delighted that they had been presented with the chance to continue the Swedish adventure alongside us. 'And Wonderful Wales are There!' was the headline in the *Evening Post*, which gave massive credit to our boss, saying: 'Jimmy Murphy has done it again! The man who stepped in after the Munich air disaster to rebuild the shattered remnants of Manchester United has now piloted Wales – "the country without a chance" – to the quarter-finals of the World Cup at their first attempt.' But Jimmy was his usual modest self and while he was probably inwardly delighted at what he achieved, he insisted that all the praise should stay with us, the players. 'Give all the credit to the boys,' he said. 'I can only tell them what to do and how wonderfully they did it.'

There wasn't too much time for patting ourselves on the back, though, because our match with Brazil was only a couple of days away. But before we headed to Gothenburg to meet the boys from the Copacabana beach all hell broke loose in the Copacabana Nightclub.

We had all been out celebrating our win against Hungary and toasting our qualification for the quarter-finals with a few drinks at the nightclub, which was attached to our hotel complex, but down a set of stairs. I know there will be people shaking their heads in disapproval at the thought of a group of footballers going out for a drink two days before they were due to face the best team in the world, but bear in mind that this was the 1950s. While we were all professionals, it was just the done thing, and nobody wanted to pass on the opportunity of a little party to celebrate what we had done. I know it wouldn't happen now and would be plastered all over the tabloids, but the reporters were actually sitting next to us having a drink and as far as they were concerned, we deserved to let our hair down a bit and relax.

It's not like we were chucking the pints down our throats, but there were one or two of the lads who probably over-indulged. John, Ivor, Cliffy and myself were at one table and Colin Webster and another group of the guys were at the table next to us. Colin had probably had a couple of drinks too many and had been taking the relaxation a bit far. I seem to remember him clambering up on to the stage at one point, grabbing hold of the microphone from the singer and loudly belting out a few songs, so he had already drawn attention to himself. He was just a really chirpy, outgoing guy and like the rest of us he felt he had something to celebrate that night. But he could also be a bit of a wind-up merchant and when the waiter came up and served John first, Colin didn't like it, saying that his table was first and that they should be served before John. The waiter shook his head and said: 'No sir, Mr Charles first', so Colin got up and thumped him. None of us could believe it. We knew Colin had sunk a few bevvies but nobody expected him to act in that way, but these things can get out of hand in the blink of an eye and the red mist had obviously come down all around him. The poor waiter went down like a sack of potatoes and a couple of his teeth came flying out.

All hell broke loose, with beer glasses flying everywhere, and a couple of the lads trying to restrain Colin. The next thing I knew, John leapt up from the table, grabbed Colin by the scruff of the neck and threw him out of the club. John was so angry, I don't think Colin's feet even touched the ground on his way to the door. All he could keep saying was: 'I didn't hit him, John. I *headed* him!'

The next morning after an impromptu meeting between the players it was decided that we should have a whip-round to pay for the damage, so we had to chip in £15 each to get the poor waiter's teeth fixed and stop him from taking further action. The management at the hotel and nightclub could have called the police in and made a big song and dance about it, but they were very fair-minded and they seemed happy enough with the whip-round we had organised. They had also been impressed with the swift action taken by John on the night, together with the sense of embarrassment felt by the rest of us. Somehow that whole sorry episode didn't really get out in the press, but this was down to the fact that some of them were sitting next to us supping when it happened.

Looking back, it's amazing that it didn't create the headlines it might have done now and our reputation somehow survived more or less unscathed. The press men that were out there with the team were all very good guys, they were like players themselves in their outlook towards life and very few of them ever had an axe to grind. They knew that we were going to fill their notebooks with a lot of good copy if they kept us on-side, so although they might have had a good 'scoop' by reporting the infamous Copacabana Nightclub incident, they knew that in the long run it made sense to hush it up. They were sports reporters, after all. They were right behind us as a team and wanted Wales to do well. Of course, the longer we stayed out at the World Cup in Sweden, the longer they stayed out too, so it was perhaps no surprise that they were rooting for us 100 per cent.

Ultimately our quarter-final clash with Brazil would end in disappointment, but when you saw what they did to the teams they played after beating us this helps keep our efforts in perspective. In the semi-finals they thumped France 5-2, in a match actually refereed by a Welshman, Benjamin Griffiths. France had the great Just Fontaine in their side and he scored 13 goals at the finals, including one against Brazil and four in the third-place play-off against West Germany. But the man who had broken our hearts, Pelé, was the main man against the French, carrying on from where he left off against Wales in Gothenburg by banging in a hat-trick. Pelé then grabbed another two goals in the final as they beat Sweden 5-2 – amazingly we had played against both of the finalists and drawn 0-0 and narrowly lost 1-0, not a bad effort in our first crack at the World Cup.

CHAPTER 11
TRANSFER TUG-OF-WAR

*'Signing for Arsenal was the most terrible choice I ever made.
I should have signed for Tottenham.'*
MEL CHARLES

THE YEARS 1958 AND 1959 were among the biggest and most important of my life. First, I got married to Vera before the World Cup and then our first child, Jeremy, was born the next year – in September 1959. The wedding was quite a big deal in Swansea because we made it a triple wedding – three Swansea Town players all getting hitched on the same day. There was no *Hello!* magazine for footballers to try and sell the pictures to back then, but nevertheless it caused a bit of a stir in the town and all the newspapers were there to record the moment. The three grooms were Don Pearson, Jeff Rees and me. You might automatically think that John would be my best man, but he was in Italy at time of the wedding, so my friend Frankie Baker stepped in to do the honours.

It was hard to be lavish or romantic in those days, even if you wanted to, and after the nuptials we all shared the train into London for a brief honeymoon and even checked into the same hotel together. If our new wives weren't too impressed with that, they didn't complain. We also had to be back at training for the Wednesday and it was all so different from the fancy overseas honeymoons people treat themselves to nowadays. Don was a wing-half with Swansea and had come through the ranks at the same time as me before he moved on to Aldershot then back to Haverfordwest, where he would become the boss. Anyway, all three of us decided to take the plunge on the same day down at the Gower, a lovely area next to the seaside on the outskirts of Swansea, in March 1958. Vera and I had some happy times during our married life, and although we later divorced in 1972, we have managed to stay good friends to this day. Vera lives just outside Swansea now and there are no hard feelings on either side, and we've even spent Christmas together.

When I got married, and with baby Jeremy on the way, my responsibilities were quickly stacking up. It dawned on me that I had to bring in as much money as I could for my family, and if I could earn more cash and get myself a more comfortable lifestyle by moving on from Swansea then I would have been a fool not to listen to offers. I would have happily stayed at Swansea from a purely football perspective, but it had already been made clear to me that there was no way the directors were going to let me stay if they could cop a decent transfer fee out of selling me, and I knew that if I dug my heels in and made a song and dance about leaving then they could put me out of the game if they wanted to. That was just the way it worked: players were there to be bought and sold, and a lot of the time they simply had to like it or lump it.

When I went back to Swansea Town after the World Cup, there was time for a bit of relaxation before pre-season training because it was summer time. While I already had a decent reputation from my first few seasons at Swansea, my performances in Sweden meant that I was starting to make more of a name for myself, and to a wider audience. My stock rose further when I was named the best centre-half to have played in the tournament and was included in FIFA's World Cup XI. At the time the World Cup all-star team was voted for by all of the journalists from the different countries who had been covering the tournament, and I was flattered to find myself in world-class company alongside the likes of Pelé, Just Fontaine, Garrincha and Manchester United's Irish goalkeeper Harry Gregg, who months earlier had been a hero during the Munich air disaster, and who would later in his career become a firm favourite down the Vetch.

It also helped my growing profile that I was John's brother, no doubt about it. John had already been a big name in world football before the finals, one of the biggest after the spectacular season he had just had with Juventus, so I guess when people learned that he had a younger brother who could play a bit as well they thought I might turn out to be just like him. It's a burden to have that kind of expectation placed on your shoulders, and unfair in many ways, but I suppose those comparisons were always going to be inevitable, and when I produced some of my best-ever performances at the finals, my profile started to soar.

The irony was that I had gone from playing at the World Cup back to the Second Division of the Football League, although the big clubs were moving in with their cheque books and the Swansea rumour-mill had again clicked into overdrive. I knew Tottenham had been tracking me for a while and their manager

Bill Nicholson made no secret of the fact that he desperately wanted to sign me as centre-half for the side he was painstakingly putting together with silverware in mind. Chelsea were also interested in bringing me to London, and so too were Arsenal. Newcastle, Manchester United and Leicester were also said to be monitoring the situation, but if I was going to leave Swansea, then it was London I fancied going to. I might have imagined that my transfer would be straightforward, but instead it degenerated into a circus. It was a long and drawn-out affair and at the end of all the wrangling it was Arsenal who eventually managed to get one over on their city rivals Spurs and Chelsea and signed me. As it turned out, signing for Arsenal was the most terrible choice I ever made.

When I was at Swansea we would do our training in the mornings, then a few of us would sometimes go down to the Castle Billiard Hall in the afternoon for a game of snooker. We'd just been going about our business, having a few frames of snooker and a laugh and a joke, when I was told that there were three First Division managers waiting to see me at the top of the stairs – Ted Drake of Chelsea, Bill Nicholson of Tottenham and Arsenal's manager George Swindin. They were practically pushing and shoving each other to get to the front of the queue at the top of those stairs to have a word with me first. They must have had their orders to win the race to sign me and didn't fancy returning from a long trip to South Wales empty-handed.

Trevor Morris was our manager at Swansea then, and he had told me that Ted Drake fancied signing me because he thought I'd be as good as John, but the truth of the matter was that I never really fancied going to Chelsea much. It probably would have been different had I gone to Tottenham, though. I think, with the benefit of hindsight, that would have been the ideal move for me, but hindsight is a wonderful thing and the fates would lead me to a different part of north London from White Hart Lane. I had been Nicholson's number one target as a centre-half, but as it turned out Dave Mackay of Hearts went there instead of me, and he didn't do too badly, did he? Tottenham won everything, with Mackay as one of their leading lights, and while I admired him as a great player, it always hurt me that it could have been me if destiny had worked differently.

I knew how close I had come to going to Tottenham and in later years I was consumed with regret, although to be fair there was a lot of pressure on me at the time and it was a difficult situation to deal with. It's hard to keep a clear head when deadlines are being set and clubs are doing all they can to woo you with promises. It wasn't ever a case of having the opportunity to sit down and mull carefully over the options in front of you, you didn't have that luxury as a player in the 1950s. I should have gone to White Hart Lane, though, no doubt about it, but it's far easier to say that now than it was at the time. All of my mates were at Tottenham, and it should have been an easy choice, but Arsenal were extremely persuasive and they also put together the best deal as far as Swansea were concerned. Even now, I have a strong bond with Arsenal, but although it will irritate some of their supporters, I think Tottenham would have been the perfect club for me.

I remember even after I'd signed for Arsenal, and we were playing Tottenham, Bill Nicholson called me into a little room where they kept all the towels and said, 'Do you still want to come to Tottenham?' There would have been hell to pay if that clandestine meeting had got out at the time, as it was a blatant attempt to tap up a player from a rival club, but there was never any danger of me telling anyone. I had far too much respect for him. He was obviously a big admirer and given what he achieved in football as arguably Tottenham's greatest-ever manager, I was, and still am, flattered that he had so much regard for me.

Bill Nicholson was a marvellous character and I feel I let him down a bit by signing for Arsenal instead. When he missed out on signing me he didn't let the grass grow under his feet; he was always one step ahead of the game. Instead of wallowing in disappointment at what was looking like a wasted trip to Swansea, he asked Trevor Morris if he could make a call from his office at the Vetch. But he wasn't phoning in the bad news to Tottenham, he was working on Plan B. He was straight on the blower to Heart of Midlothian up in Edinburgh to enquire about signing their promising central defender Dave Mackay – and apparently he never paid Trevor a penny for that call either! He was a fast thinker, true enough, and in getting Mackay from Hearts he had pulled off a masterstroke, as history shows now.

My transfer from Swansea was an emotionally draining experience and I was back-page news every day of the week as the drama unfolded. It all started to come to a head when I asked the club if I could have a part-time job outside football to give me more of an income. It was an idea they had raised with me in the past and it seemed like everyone would be a winner – I would get to stay at Swansea and they would keep their captain. The wages were capped at £14 a week at the Swans, with no room for negotiation, and the way I saw it if I could get another job it would give me just enough to stay with Swansea rather than having to go and sign for someone else.

I reckoned that, as an international who had played in the World Cup, I was entitled to First Division wages, and for a while Swansea told me they were going to set me up as manager of a garage to help complement what I was already earning at the

Vetch. But although they kept promising that they would fix something up, nothing ever materialised and it came to the stage where I told them to put up or shut up. When I was met with a stony silence, I had no option but to hand in a transfer request because I already knew that there were a few clubs who were keen on signing me. There was another problem to throw into the mix too – the Football League were having kittens when they heard about my request for a part-time job, as they were worried it would open the floodgates, with dozens of other players ready to sit up and take notice and hand in similar requests. The League made it clear in no uncertain terms that they would do everything in their power to oppose the idea.

I was the first player to have something resembling an 'agent', a local solicitor called Neil Harris, who I employed for the transfer only. He was loosely described as my 'business manager' in the newspapers, but he was given the cold shoulder by all of the clubs involved and the Football League, who were very suspicious of any so-called outsider becoming involved in any negotiations. Transfers were usually completed after a bit of haggling between the clubs concerned. There were never any middle men or agents back then, so for me to hire Harris was a bit of a ground-breaking move. Not that it really did me much good. For the privilege of signing for the mighty Arsenal, all I got was a £20 signing-on fee. I can still picture the money now – four crisp old fivers! And the thing was, I remember being pretty made up with that at the time; I thought it was a bit of a result. We didn't really know much about money in those days. My wages at Swansea had been £14 a week during the season, and then £12 in the summer. But out of that £14 you still had to pay rent and all your other outgoings. I started off on £16 a week at Arsenal then went up to £20 – no wonder I'm skint now. I think

Patrick Vieira and Thierry Henry probably made £20 in less than a minute during their time at Arsenal.

The actual signing talks with Arsenal were a bit unusual. We decided it would make sense to meet somewhere away from London or Swansea, and so we chose a quiet café in Cowbridge, a little town in the Vale of Glamorgan. When I went up there to speak to George Swindin, he had his captain Tommy Docherty with him to help add weight to his powers of persuasion, along with Peter Davies and Dave Dodson, the two Arsenal reserves who were central to the deal going ahead as a cash-plus-player transfer.

Dave Dodson had never even been to Wales before, so I thought I would take the opportunity to play some mind games with him, to test whether he really did want to go through with the move. When I got a chance I followed him to the toilet and asked for a quick word. I said to him: 'Dave, have you ever been to Swansea?' When he said no, I said: 'It's all bloody coal mines there, you don't want to be going there – it's a rotten place. It's not for you, Dave, I would steer well clear if I was you'. I tried to put him off because if he had backed out the deal might have been off and I would have been able to wriggle out of it! But it was just my luck that Peter Davies was from Llanelli and he was dying to get back to Wales.

Tommy Docherty had come down with George to help seal the deal and together they put over a passionate case for me to move to Arsenal. After the meeting at Cowbridge I was still none the wiser as to whether the deal between Arsenal and Swansea would be done or not, but I didn't have to wait long to find out. The very next morning at nine o'clock I got a knock at the door and the physio, Bernard Sherington, was standing there. He said: 'Mel, you have to come to Cardiff with me today.' I said, 'What for?' and he said, 'You're going there to sign for Arsenal.' No arguments, no more negotiations, nothing, I was just told to get my coat on because I was going to Arsenal. A knock at the door and you're gone, away to a new club.

The wheels had been set in motion on 9 March 1959, when Swansea formally decided Mel Charles was up for sale to the highest bidder. This is how it panned out on a day-to-day basis, with the following reports appearing in the sports pages of the *South Wales Evening Post*. With hardly any television sets in the town, it was the closest thing to a soap opera...

9 March
SWANSEA TOWN SAY MEL CAN GO

Swansea Town manager Trevor Morris has been given a free hand to deal with Mel Charles' application for a transfer and the club has agreed to his request, but on their terms. Their hands have been forced by Charles' insistence that he wants a part-time job outside his contract and that he wishes to play First Division football. In an interview with the manager today Charles repeated these demands. An official statement released by the club today said: 'In view of all the relevant circumstances, we feel that we should accede to Charles' request for a transfer. Naturally we are talking a record fee, but we would much prefer a cash plus player deal in preference to a straight cash transaction because it is essential that we should get the right replacements. There are half-a-dozen clubs whom we have pledged to notify. They have been acquainted of the position and it is now up to them.' Manager Morris today contacted the clubs who have shown an interest in the Swans skipper. Among them are Arsenal, Chelsea, Newcastle, Tottenham and Manchester United, even though Matt Busby has publicly stated that he does not intend signing any new men this season. One thing is certain — if the club does not get a satisfactory deal Charles will stay at the Vetch.

10 March

LEAGUE HAND OUT A WARNING – DEMAND FOR PART-TIME JOB ASKING FOR TROUBLE

Swansea Town's decision to grant Mel Charles' request for a transfer has taken a new turn. Football League president Mr Joe Richards has warned that any player requesting a part-time job outside football is asking for trouble. There seems little doubt that the League is watching the position closely. There is a question of principle involved and if Swansea Town had agreed to Charles' request for a part-time job they would only have opened the way for other players to ask for the same consideration. The League has made it clear that any provision of a part-time job is illegal. Charles' reaction to Swansea Town's official statement, published first in the Evening Post, has not been favourable. 'It is ridiculous,' he said. 'No player is worth £50,000. I put my value at half that figure and if Swansea persist in asking for £50,000 I shall take the matter to the League. Swansea Town manager Trevor Morris said today: 'The position is perfectly clear. Charles and his behind-the-scenes advisors asked for a transfer and forced us into acceding to it. We reserve the right to put our own valuation on him. If we don't get it Charles stays and that's that.' In the meantime, Arsenal and Tottenham have made enquiries. Mr George Swindin, the Arsenal chief, was stated this morning to be on his way to Swansea. 'I am not interested in anything like a £50,000 fee,' he said, 'but we are prepared to do business on a player exchange basis.' Tottenham, who already have two former Swans stars Terry Medwin and Cliff Jones on their staff, are holding a special meeting today and are sure to make a bid for Charles. Leicester City manager Mike Gillus has made an offer of £20,000 plus one of five players.

11 March

NOW CHELSEA JOIN IN – TED DRAKE MAKES THE TRIP TO THE VETCH FIELD

Chelsea joined the Mel Charles race today and their manager Ted Drake arrived at the Vetch Field late this afternoon. The London club, who have not entered the transfer market for some time, should have plenty to offer in exchange for the Welsh international. Apart from the cash side – which should not present too much of a headache to the wealthy Pensioners – they have several players whom they could offer in exchange. Swansea had a bird's eye last week of the men Chelsea might offer, for the latter club's reserve side won 3-2 at the Vetch Field. Meanwhile, Arsenal are not letting the grass grow under their feet. Today, in the absence of their manager George Swindin, who left for Nottingham with his reserves side, secretary Bob Wall stated: 'Mr Swindin discussed various aspects of the transfer with Swansea Town manager Trevor Morris. Our board will now consider the matter and dependent on their consideration within the next few days we may decide to make a firm offer.'

12 March

SPURS ARE THE FAVOURITES – ARSENAL, SAYS CHARLES, BUT THE TOTTENHAM BID TOPS THE LOT

Although Mel Charles has stated that he wants to be transferred to Arsenal, Tottenham Hotspur came in this morning with what is a far more attractive bid and are favourites to obtain the Swansea Town player. Spurs manager Bill Nicholson, who already has two former Swansea players on his books in Terry Medwin and Cliff Jones, is on his way to Swansea. He will offer a player who is in the first-team, plus a substantial fee. There seems little doubt that the two clubs will come to terms. Arsenal are, of course, in the field. They have made a straight cash offer of £35,000, plus a couple of young players. In the meantime, George Swindin, accompanied by Tommy Docherty, took the opportunity of seeing Charles and had a long chat with the player and his wife at his home. 'I very much want Charles as a centre-half so that I can build my team around him,' said Swindin. 'I have wanted him for a long time and I am not worried about the deadline for signing.' Charles had this to say of his chat with Mr Swindin: 'He has more or less talked me into going to Arsenal. I won't go anywhere but Arsenal. Nothing will change my mind.'

13 March: MEL CHARLES ADAMANT – SO NOW IT'S DEADLOCK

Unless Mel Charles changes his mind today, he will remain with Swansea Town. He had a two-hour talk with Spurs manager Bill Nicholson last night but remained adamant about wanting to go to Arsenal. 'I told Mr Nicholson that I had made up my mind to go to Arsenal,' said Charles. 'It's always been my ambition to join them.' Manager Trevor Morris has not changed his views either: 'Tottenham made the best offer, which we accepted. Newcastle United were last in with an offer of a cheque plus centre-forward Curry and full-back McKinney, but Mr Charlie Mitten, the Newcastle manager, was told we had already agreed to Tottenham's terms.'

The Tottenham offer was obviously the one that appealed most to the club, but on 14 March they got sick of waiting. Bill Nicholson made his famous phone call to Hearts and instead signed Dave Mackay instead as the perfect alternative. Spurs had officially lost interest because I'd already gone on record as saying that the Arsenal bid appealed to me more.

While this transfer tug-of-war raged on I was still doing my best to concentrate on football and playing for the Swans. That month, we recorded a famous win against Cardiff at Ninian Park, recording Swansea's first-ever league win at the ground and our first-ever league goal. Mel Nurse, who was only 21 at the time, had the honour of scoring that historic goal from the penalty spot and it was enough for us to win 1-0. At least I had been on a winning team for my final derby in a Swansea shirt. It wasn't exactly a dream end to my time at the club though, because we went up to Middlesbrough and were played off the park, losing 6-2. I played at centre-forward, but was totally eclipsed by Brian Clough, who scored four for Boro, including three in the first half.

With Tottenham out of the running, the path was more or less clear for Arsenal, although my business manager Harris was still keen to set up a meeting with Newcastle United and the Football League on Good Friday to hear what they had to offer. The Football League had made him a sworn enemy by that stage though, and they released a statement from secretary Alan Hardacre which read: 'The Football League is not interested in meeting Mr. Neil Harris. As far as the League is concerned he has nothing to do with the transfer of any Football League player. Not in any circumstances would the League meet him.'

Newcastle knew that they were chasing a lost cause though, and when Arsenal came back with a new, improved offer and threw a couple of players into the mix, the deal was well and truly swung in their favour. Their offer was Peter Davies and Dave Dodson, together with a then-British record transfer fee of £42,750, and that was enough for Swansea to decide to make it a done deal. Dave Dodson was an ex-England youth winger and he ended up scoring 11 goals in 30 games at Swansea before he was sold to Portsmouth for £4,000 in December 1961. Things

137

worked out a little better at the Vetch for Peter Davies, who helped the Swans win the Welsh Cup in 1961 and played 134 league games for the club. He moved on to Brighton in July 1965 and also played in South Africa later in his career, but he came back to live in Swansea and ran a few pubs around town, including the Bay View on Oystermouth Road.

After a mad month of transfer wrangling, I finally had closure and I signed for Arsenal on 31 March 1959.

Leaving Swansea was a wrench, but the truth was that a combination of circumstances forced me to go to Arsenal. You didn't have the bargaining power at your disposal as a player back then as you do now. The situation had escalated so quickly that I had to go, or Swansea could have reacted badly to having a contract rebel on their hands, and decided to put me out of football. It didn't help either that I had a manager who was hell-bent on being in control of the transfer. There were times during the negotiations when Trevor Morris was a real pain in the backside to deal with, and he was more intent on getting his way than me getting mine. He was a remarkably stubborn man and tried to play hard-ball throughout; he treated me like a commodity rather than a person. I think his record as a 'selling' manager, rather than one who wanted to build and nurture a good team, speaks for itself – seven internationals left the Vetch during his time in charge, and while he might have brought in a few quid for Swansea, there's no doubt the fans would have preferred to see their favourites stay put.

Try as I might, throughout my career I could never shake off the nagging feeling of what might have been had I decided to go to Tottenham instead of Arsenal. At that time Tottenham already had Cliffy Jones and Terry Medwin at the club, and another one of my international team-mates, Mel Hopkins, who they had signed from the famous Ystrad Boys Club in Rhondda. It was a shame for Mel Hopkins: he missed out on the Double season with Spurs because he had smashed his nose in a game against Scotland in a collision with Ian St John. It was a hell of a mess after that, a really bad one that put him out for months – I think he still felt a shiver run up his nose every time he saw Saint and Greavsie on the box because of that!

In Cliffy's case things could not have gone better for him at White Hart Lane – he was something of a legend with Spurs. He played 300-odd times for them after signing from the Swans in 1958 and got more than 100 goals, a fantastic scoring record for a winger. He might have had all the glory at Spurs, but he still says his time at Swansea was the best of his life. We're still great mates to this day. The same applies to Terry, who also had a great career at Tottenham. He went there from Swansea for £25,000 in 1956 and helped them win the double in 1961 and then another FA Cup in 1962, but then he broke his leg the year after that and that forced him to retire.

But while I often wonder how it would have worked out with Spurs, I'm probably wasting my time dwelling on the past. It was Arsenal who signed me and despite my numerous ups and downs at Highbury, I'm still very fond of them to this day. When I get the newspaper or watch the results coming in on television, straightaway I look out for all my old clubs, and that includes Arsenal. I get a lot of stick about my Arsenal connection from some of the punters in my local boozer, the Badminton Bar in the Sandfields area of Swansea. You'll get folk that support every other club under the sun trying to wind me up about Arsenal, and I've got a running bet with the barmaid, who is a mad-keen Liverpool fan. Every time Liverpool and Arsenal are playing, it's a straight bet between her and me of one pint to the team who does best. She'll say otherwise, but I'd say I'm well ahead on the number of pints I've won at her expense – I think I must owe one or two of them to Arsène Wenger!

Arsenal are still a great club, but there's no doubt they have changed beyond all recognition from the team that I signed for in 1959. They were always a club with a great tradition, but they didn't have the cosmopolitan flair that guys like Wenger, Thierry Henry and Patrick Vieira have brought them in recent years. The new batch of kids that Wenger is bringing through now look a bit special too, and it's good to see them up near the top of the league every season because as I know only too well that wasn't always the case. They've also moved away from Highbury, of course, and while I loved the old ground and its unique atmosphere, I wouldn't mind seeing what the Emirates Stadium is like, just to compare the two. I'm not a fan of the shiny, new grounds, but I'll always have a place in my heart for Arsenal, and it was an honour to have played for them.

CHAPTER 12
HIGHBURY HIGH LIFE

'Highbury was a grand, but intimidating place. The moment you set foot inside the stadium you got an instant buzz.'
MEL CHARLES

ARSENAL TREATED ME fantastically well when I first arrived. They found me a beautiful detached house in Southgate, a nice suburb in the Enfield borough of north London. I think I could have bought the house at the time for about £3,000, but never did, as the club sorted out the rent. I was on £20 a week but Arsenal took care of things like the house and car, which made a big difference. The house had lots of room and a lovely garden, and it was perfect for Vera and Jeremy, who was born not long after the Arsenal deal went through. I wouldn't let Vera have Jeremy in England, though. I wanted him to be born in Swansea and be a true Welshman, so I sent her home and she had him in Morriston Hospital in my home town, Swansea.

On £20 a week, I may not have been getting paid much in

actual wages, but Arsenal and their supporters always looked after me very well, helping out whatever way they could, and there were plenty of little perks to make up for anything that was lacking in my wage packet. Some of the Arsenal-supporting shopkeepers would happily give us baby clothes and prams and so on, and they were always very kind towards me and my young family. I was one of the first players lucky enough to get a car, a little red-and-white Standard, and I would give my team-mates a lift to training in it. I made them give me money for petrol mind you, about £1 a week, and I got some stick for that. They used to have a right go at me for charging them, calling me a Scrooge and a tight-arse, but I wasn't one for letting them get something for nothing, and petrol wasn't cheap either. I could feel my ears burning from time to time though, because they used to begrudge handing over any money to me, and it became a running joke among some of my mates about my tightness. Getting ferried around in a car was still a bit of a novelty then, and they were prepared to pay their way to get a lift from me.

After the Standard I drove about in a Sunbeam Talbot, which was also red and white – well, what other colours would you pick if you played for Arsenal? My number plate was a bit flash – MEL 9 – so you could say I was noticed wherever I went. That number plate would be worth a fortune now, but I didn't recognise its value at the time and when it came to selling the car, I sold the plates too, which wasn't the most clever thing to do. People pay about ten grand for plates like that now.

Highbury itself was a grand, but intimidating place. The moment you set foot inside the stadium you got an instant buzz; there was an air of authority surrounding the place. When you walked through the front door into the reception area you immediately knew you were at a football club with real status. In the foyer, next to a sweeping flight of stairs, they had a big bronze bust of Herbert Chapman, the legendary manager who had been a pioneer in English football during his many years as the governor at Highbury. It dominated the room so much, you almost felt like the right thing to do would be to bow in front of it. No expense was spared at Highbury, and the players and staff lived in a certain amount of luxury. It was the first time I had ever experienced central heating under the floorboards. When I was down at the Vetch we had an old wooden floor and all you would get from that was freezing cold feet and splinters, so to put your feet on a warm floor was cutting-edge technology to me!

George Swindin was the manager throughout my time with Arsenal and he was all right to have as your boss, a decent guy that you could trust and turn to, if you needed a quiet word in his ear. He had been a great goalkeeper for Arsenal himself after joining the club from Bradford and he went on to win a few league championships as a player. But he found himself under great pressure to cut it as a manager at Highbury. While George was easy-going and no problem to get on with, his assistant Ron Greenwood was the one that I didn't like; he absolutely dumbfounded me at times.

I know Ron did very well as a coach and manager, and wouldn't wish to take anything away from his achievements in the game, but I had quite a few run-ins with him and I think he was the type of guy who wasn't really one to forgive and forget. Our personalities clashed from the moment I met him and he made no secret of the fact that he didn't like me. I think he preferred the type of player who was willing to do exactly as he said, and if you had a big personality and you liked a laugh and a joke, he took it the wrong way and thought you were not taking him seriously enough.

I remember one funny incident when Greenwood was coach

that saw things come to a head between the pair of us. We were up at Old Trafford for an away match against Manchester United and he started off on one of his long-winded tactical talks in the changing room. It was really warm in there and he was talking so much that I could feel my eyelids start to get heavy and eventually I fell asleep in the corner. I must have only dozed off for a minute or two, if as long as that. He was working his way through the team one by one and issuing instructions from Jack Kelsey, then the defenders and so on. I was due to be playing centre forward that day, so I was last in line to get issued with Ron's words of wisdom, and I must have sensed he was getting close to me because I woke up with a start when he was virtually standing over me. I was still feeling a bit woozy, but I could hear him saying to me: 'Mel, I want you to mark Space!' I looked at the sheet of paper he was holding up in front of me, full of squiggles, names and diagrams, read up and down his list, and all I could blurt out was: 'But he's not even playing, Ron!' The rest of the lads were falling about killing themselves with laughter, and couldn't believe I had been daft enough to think United had a new player called Space in their side. Ron, on the other hand, didn't see the funny side. He didn't like me, especially after that.

I remember another time on the training ground when Ron was asking me to make a 'blind-side run'. I just gave him a blank look, nothing but confusion registering on my face. I didn't know WHAT to do and didn't have the foggiest what he was banging on about. Just before we were about to be put through the training drill, I went up to him, and because I was still a bit bamboozled with all this 'blind-side' talk, I asked him, quite innocently: 'Ron, how can I see with my eyes shut?'. He would use all the latest coaching jargon, but it would just drive me up the wall. I wasn't really one for delving too deep into tactics; I liked to keep it simple. Ron Greenwood, on the other hand, lapped it all up. He would talk about 'wall-passes' when it was a plain old one-two to me. George was a straight-talker, but he left all the tactical explanations to Ron, and he was an incredibly dour man to deal with.

Training could be tough at Arsenal too. We didn't run all the time; the worst part I remember about training was actually the walking, which we did a lot. I was always at the back of the pack, and some of the endurance work used to leave me bloody knackered. Safe to say I was not the model trainer, although because I was quite naturally fit, I always felt fit enough to do myself justice on a Saturday before the injuries started to interfere.

Arsenal were always trying to embrace new technology and they even experimented with giving us earpieces so we could receive instructions during training – that may not sound too state-of-the-art now, but remember, this was 50-odd years ago, and man was still 10 years away from walking on the moon! Usually I just let football come naturally to me, and didn't respond very well to too much coaching; it would only make my head spin. So when they had us all wired up and invited a whole load of photographers and journalists down to watch the experiment, I was a bit out of my depth. Ron was obviously eager to impress the watching reporters and was barking instructions through the earpiece like nobody's business, telling me to do this and that, but after a couple minutes of him buzzing in my ear like an angry insect, I tore the stupid thing out of my ear and trampled it into the ground. He asked me what the problem was and I told him straight: 'I'm so bloody confused getting all these instructions that I don't even know which way I'm supposed to be kicking.'

George, on the other hand, was fine, and although there were games I simply shouldn't have been playing due to the knee injuries I suffered during my time at Highbury, I couldn't blame him for picking me. He was only following orders from a board of directors determined to get as much value for money from the cash they had shelled out on me. I was a high-profile, expensive signing, and if I was constantly on the sidelines then they felt they would come under fire from the Arsenal supporters. My welfare didn't really come into the equation.

George was a fairly gruff Yorkshireman, and he had been a no-nonsense PT instructor in Germany during the war, but you always knew where you stood with him. He wouldn't pussy-foot around, and I respected that. He had been a great keeper for Arsenal for years, before Jack Kelsey took his place, and when he took over as manager at Highbury in the summer of 1958, he had a tough job on his hands because the club were a little down in the dumps after failing to build on the league titles and cups they had won only a few years earlier. There was a lot of talent at Arsenal when I first went there, guys like Tommy Docherty, David Herd, Vic Groves and Bill Dodgin, but while they were all very good players I don't think any of them were quite as good as some of my team-mates in the Welsh international side, who I rated as world-class – Ivor Allchurch and John, for starters. Dave Bowen, who had captained Wales at the 1958 World Cup and was one of the best motivators I ever saw on the park, had been one of the main men at Arsenal when I arrived, but no sooner was I in the door than he was off to Northampton Town as player-manager for £7,000, back to the club from which he had joined Arsenal in 1950 for £1,000.

In the weeks before I signed for The Gunners, the team suffered a disastrous month in the First Division, failing to win a single game, and their hopes of winning the title were effectively crushed when they lost 6-1 away at Wolves, who proved themselves worthy champions that year, scoring 110 goals in their 42 games. By the time I arrived there were only seven fixtures left of the 1958/59 season, and our form picked up a bit, losing only one of those matches to Birmingham. We managed to finish with three straight wins, winning up at Blackpool before giving the Arsenal fans some optimism for the following campaign with back-to-back wins at Highbury against Portsmouth and Birmingham to finish a respectable third in the league.

I actually made my Highbury debut in a friendly match against Glasgow Rangers, and the fans made me very welcome. The most passionate part of the ground at Highbury was the North Bank, just like Swansea, and they could make a hell of a noise. Arsenal's big rivals Tottenham finished only 18th that season, but the Nicholson revolution was already under way and in the new manager's first match in charge they beat Everton 10-4 to give an early warning that they would soon be a force to be reckoned with.

We started the 1959/60 season with a disappointing defeat at home to Sheffield Wednesday, but opening games are always really difficult and it's never fair to judge a team on their first match. When you have gone through all the hard training during summer, maybe you're just a little bit too tense and nervous by the time the first match comes around, and that was the case against Sheffield Wednesday, who were a good side that year and finished in the top five. We may have lost 1-0, which was disappointing in front of our own fans, but we played well enough, and there was no suggestion of anyone rushing to press the panic button. In fact, after that opening-game blip we went on an unbeaten league run of nine games, and although a few of them were draws, we found ourselves up with the pace. But October was a shocker for us and we lost three on the spin, away to Everton and Manchester United, and at home to Preston.

Worse was to follow, because in the run-up to Christmas we lost five in a row, including a couple of thumping away defeats up at Newcastle and Sheffield Wednesday. We had another one of those crazy double-headers, kindly dreamt up by the Football League, where we played Luton twice in three days – we lost 3-0 at home on Boxing Day, but redeemed ourselves in the return, winning 1-0. Confidence was starting to ebb away, and the fans were getting a bit agitated because Tottenham were beginning to look the part and climbing up the league under Nicholson.

I remember making a real fool of myself on television after one of my early games for Arsenal. We had been playing under our floodlights and sometimes the glare would play havoc with my eyes. *Match of the Day* wasn't given a regular slot until later in the 1960s, but already the BBC were starting to experiment with showing some football highlights now and again, and they had the cameras down at Highbury for this particular game.

The interviewer managed to grab a word with me at the end of the game, and after asking me a couple of questions, he noticed my eyes were streaming and asked me if I was all right. I meant to tell him that it was cataracts that were making my eyes play up, but I got all tongue tied and to my eternal embarrassment I said to him: 'Yeah, I'm okay, I've just got clitorises on my eyes!' You should have seen the look on his face; he was speechless.

All of his crew started falling about pissing themselves at me and they couldn't even hold the television camera for shaking with laughter. The thing was, I didn't even know the word or what one was! I must have just heard it from one of the lads one day and it had stuck in my mind for some reason. I still blush about that slip-up now. It's safe to say that my appearances on TV became limited after that incident – I think they would seek out any Arsenal player but me!

Our first match of 1960 was a home game against champions Wolves, who were going great guns again and would eventually finish runners-up as well as winning the FA Cup. We thought we might have turned the corner when we fought out a 4-4 draw in the league, but our involvement in the FA Cup proved to be a major embarrassment for us. We drew 2-2 away at Rotherham and were fancied to brush them aside in the replay. But we could only manage a 1-1 draw at Highbury and then we mucked up the second replay, which had to be played at a neutral Hillsborough, and lost 2-0. That at least spurred us on to play a bit in the league and we won five out of our next six games. Importantly for my confidence I was finding the net regularly, scoring in a 2-1 win at Man City before getting my first-ever Arsenal hat-trick in a brilliant 5-2 win over Blackburn Rovers at home on 6 February.

I could, and should, have made it two Highbury hat-tricks in a row when we met Everton a fortnight later, but I blew my big chance. I had scored two and was playing out of my skin when I was bundled over face-down in the mud to win a penalty. I picked myself up and went charging over for the ball to take the spot-kick myself. It was a really horrible, muddy pitch and I could feel my legs starting to slip and slide as I took my run-up. By the time I got to the ball my balance was all over the place and I just duffed the ball towards the goal. It was a real trundler and it barely made it to the six-yard box. I think the Everton keeper Jimmy O'Neill could hardly believe his luck, but he barely had to move to bend down and pick my pathetic effort out of the muck. We still beat them 2-1, mind you, and I had turned in a decent game, so there was no harm done apart from me messing up the chance to steal all the glory with a hat-trick.

While I was managing to score quite a few goals, and the fans were being kind enough towards me, I wasn't all that pleased with my overall form at Arsenal. I was finding it a bit hard to settle and my price tag weighed heavily on me at times. Also, I was struggling a bit with a wife and a young kid to support in a strange city, and the social scene among the players wasn't a patch on what I had been used to at Swansea.

Before my pal George Eastham was signed by Arsenal in 1960, I suppose I was closest at Highbury to my Wales international team-mate Jack Kelsey, another man with a connection to my home town as he had started his football career with the Swansea league club, Winch Wen. Like most goalkeepers he was a bit of an eccentric and would sometimes put chewing gum on his gloves to make the ball stick. He was a great character with a dry sense of humour and a sense of mischief, but he was essentially a loner, and although we were fellow countrymen, a lot of the time we did our own thing. Jack would have his 300 fags for the weekend and just kept himself to himself. That didn't mean that he wasn't game for a laugh, although I wish he had kept himself to himself on one particular ill-fated business venture he got me mixed up in.

I think he saw me as a bit of a soft touch and he enjoyed a few practical jokes at my expense, but on that occasion, the joke was on both of us. We were going out to Russia for a game and Kelsey shuffled up to me, acting all shifty, and said, 'Hey, Mel, there's a fortune to be made out there, just do as I say! Get yourself two hundred quid together and we will make a killing, the easiest money you have ever made'. I was a sucker for the prospect of making a fast buck, and while two hundred quid was a tidy outlay in those days, I decided it was well worth the gamble for some easy money, especially if it was as simple as Kelsey was making out. Jack explained the plan further, telling me, 'The Russians can't get any nylons, they can't get razor blades and they can't get milk chocolate, so we'll take out as much as we can, satisfy the demand and make ourselves a tidy profit.'

So I got the cash together, gave it to him and we bought up as much chocolate, razors and as many pairs of tights as we could – two hundred pounds' worth a head. Our cases were crammed full of the stuff and we were looking forward to cashing in on our own personal sideline to make us a few bob. As soon as we got the chance in Russia, we grabbed a table at the train station, opened our suitcases and started to flog our wares. They were selling like hot cakes and within an hour we had shifted the lot. We must have looked like Del Boy and Rodney down the market as we flogged our chocolate and nylons, and some of the Russians were barging and pushing each other to be first in the queue, thrusting money at us. Eventually we ended up with piles of roubles stuffed into our pockets and our suitcases were empty in no time at all.

Kelsey was all chuffed with himself and was saying to me, 'I told you it was easy money, Mel!' I had a massive grin on my face too, and thought my luck was in. There was one small problem we hadn't expected, though – when we got back to Britain and we tried to go to the bank to cash the roubles, they wouldn't change them for sterling! They were worthless unless we ever happened to go back to Russia, and that wasn't very likely. We had made a cock-up of epic proportions. I've still got some of those bloody roubles to this day and I can hardly bear to even look at them. We had lost two hundred quid each – as Del Boy might say… what a pair of plonkers!

'Mel Charles, the massive Welshman who carries a £43,500 price tag and the ceaseless worry of injury, faces 90 minutes which

CHAPTER 13

WOUNDED GUNNER

could make or break his First Division future.'
DAILY EXPRESS, 31 DECEMBER 1960

WHEN I STARTED TO SUFFER problems with my knee I suppose that was the beginning of the end of my time at Highbury. Ask any footballer what frustrates them most in the game, and 99 out of 100 will tell you that it's injuries, and missing matches because you're on the treatment table. At Swansea, I had been incredibly lucky to limit my time on the sidelines to one knee cartilage injury, but I started to suffer ligament trouble in both knees when I was at Arsenal. I suppose a lot of it had to do with the positions that I was played in. At centre-half or centre-forward there's no hiding place from the rougher side of the game, and I was never the type to shirk a tackle. I went in where it hurt, and boy it hurt sometimes; I needed my knees to be functioning at full power to win balls in the air, and when I started to develop niggling problems, this definitely had an effect on my game.

While Arsenal had signed me on the strength of what I had done at the World Cup at centre-half, George Swindin generally preferred to use me as a centre-forward. They wanted me to do what John was doing over in Italy and score goals. I was always happier playing at right-half if the chance arose, but Arsenal rarely played me there and saw me more as a striker, with the simple brief to score goals. I didn't mind getting switched around all the time. As long as I was on the field, that was the most important thing for me – unless I was bandaged up like a mummy, that is.

I should have been given a decent rest, to allow the knee injuries to heal properly, but Arsenal had other ideas. I accept they didn't have the medical technology at their disposal then that they do now, but to me it looked like common sense to take it easy and give me a bit of time to recover. But Arsenal felt that because I was their most expensive signing, I should be out on the pitch at all costs and if there was any way of patching me up, they would find it. At the end of some games I would be in agony, but I was the type of guy who felt I would be letting them down if I didn't at least try and give it a go. There were no subs to ride to the rescue either; they weren't introduced to the Football League until the 1965/66 season. In my day, once you were named in that starting eleven, you had to make damn sure you lasted the game or your team was in trouble – you would be letting the side down if you limped off. So I was stuck in a Catch-22 situation, even though I knew I was doing myself some damage. The physios were doing everything to make sure I could play: splitting my knees to get the pus out, whatever it took to get me out on the pitch. They would sit six heated jam jars on my knee on the Friday to ease the swelling and make sure I could play. All I needed was a month off to recover, but I had no chance of getting a rest.

I remember one match when we played against Newcastle, who had Ivor Allchurch in their side. My leg was heavily bandaged and I was wincing in agony, and it did not escape Ivor's attention that I was limping even as we ran out the tunnel together. He said: 'Mel, what the hell are you playing for? You can hardly walk, never mind run!' But I couldn't really give him an answer. I was one of the highest-priced footballers in Britain and George Swindin was under pressure to play me. I had no option at all. You had an allegiance to the club. Ivor was looking out for me that day, but while I appreciated his concern, your club was your bread and butter, and you just couldn't do anything about it, you just had to get on with it.

The fact that I was suffering a few setbacks with my injuries in the 1960/61 season was not helped by the growing success of our arch-rivals Spurs, who were the best team by far that year. The Arsenal fans didn't like that one bit and they started to get a bit edgy at the matches, with more pressure heaped on us to deliver the goods as a result.

We blew hot and cold in the early weeks of the season, and I was already starting to miss a game here and there with my knee. The first north London derby of the season was at Highbury in September and we lost 3-2 in a cracking match. Just as it had been during my time at Swansea, the problem was consistency and we could swing wildly from one extreme to another. For instance, we ran Newcastle into the ground at Highbury, beating them 5-0, but then a few weeks later we turned in an abysmal performance to lose 6-0 at West Ham.

Defeats to any of our London rivals understandably never went down well with the fans, and when we followed up that Hammers hammering with a 4-1 defeat to Chelsea, who still had

Jimmy Greaves scoring goals for fun, the knives were out for us. A few eyes turned to me, because I was the most expensive player on the books, and I must admit that it did affect me. I had come from Swansea, where I was used to people always giving me a pat on the back and boosting my confidence, to a big club like Arsenal where you had to take the rough with the smooth if results weren't going your way. At times like that I felt a long way from home.

The frustration I was experiencing with my injuries and the stop-start nature of my season was adequately summed up on the back page of the *Daily Express* in their New Year's Eve edition. The article, by Clive Toye, read:

MEL CHARLES…MAN IN FEAR – IT'S MAKE OR BREAK FOR ARSENAL STAR AS 1960 DIES

Mel Charles, the massive Welshman who carries a £43,500 price tag and the ceaseless worry of injury, faces 90 minutes which could make or break his First Division future. Charles – the man as familiar with the operating table as he is with Highbury's playing pitch since Arsenal poured out cash for him – has had only four post-operation League games. All of them have been at centre-forward. Today he plays at Nottingham Forest as centre-half, surrounded by an inexperienced, youthful Arsenal defence. Behind him he has young Irish backs Ted Magill and Bily McCullough. On his right is young Irishman Terry Neill. Only goalkeeper Jack Kelsey and skipper Vic Groves are experienced men from whom he can expect help. Forest, without a defeat in their last eight games, are sure to keep Charles twisting and turning to halt them. Only recently Charles admitted: 'My knee is still suspect. It's painful when I twist quickly'. Arsenal manager George Swindin then decided to end the Charles risk of centre-forward acrobatics by putting him at right half. Yet mighty Mel – because of the

Christmas injury to first choice John Snedden – is flung now into the equally risky spot of centre-half.

I couldn't have been that risky because we went up to play Forest that day and won 5–3. They had players like Bobby McKinlay, Colin Booth and Jack Burkitt in their side, and had taken 14 points from 16 in the eight games before they met us, so to go up there with a young side and score five goals was a great effort. Our euphoria wasn't to last long, though. We got knocked out of the FA Cup at the first hurdle again, losing up at Sunderland, and when Tottenham beat us 4–2 at White Hart Lane not long after the New Year, we knew that we were heading for a barren season with no trophies to show for our efforts. Spurs, on the other hand, had done the double over us and were well on their way to winning a famous league and cup Double. And yes, I admit it; I kept thinking to myself over and over again, 'That could have been me!'

As we stuttered our way to the end of the season, uncomfortably in the shadow of our neighbours, we managed to lose the last three games to Chelsea, Wolves and Everton. I think it's fair to say that our fans were sick of the sight of us, and suddenly George Swindin's coat was on a shaky peg as well. It had been a really disappointing season, and after finishing 11th, we finished 25 points between Tottenham, who really rammed our underachievement down our throats by becoming the first club in the 20th century to win the League and Cup Double.

The one silver lining of that season was the signing of George Eastham from Newcastle, one of the best transfer moves Arsenal ever made, although the deal itself was mired in controversy. The two of us became great friends; we just seemed to hit it off right away. Team spirit at Arsenal was sometimes lacking because

157

London is such an enormous place and our houses were scattered far apart. I'd come from a small town like Swansea, where team-mates could socialise and become a close-knit group but London, as you would expect, was completely different. As a team we hardly ever went out for a drink together, but the one I would always go out for a drink with after training or after a game was George because we lived quite close together. Sometimes Kelsey used to come too, but he had a car and often went his own way. George was my room-mate on any overnight away trips with Arsenal, while Cliffy Jones had the dubious pleasure of sharing with me when we were away with Wales. George was a great character, a marvellous mate to be knocking about with. We had some laughs together and the pair of us were like Mutt and Jeff.

I remember one game with Arsenal when we went up for an overnight stay in Blackpool for a match against Burnley. We were staying in a little hotel with all mod cons – a swimming pool, a games room with snooker and so on. To pass the time we would organise ourselves into pairs and play doubles, then have individual tournaments too, just a bit of fun to while away the time. But you do get a little bored after a while with all the clean-cut games and sometimes you found you were unable to help yourself trying to create a bit of excitement. So George and I sneaked out to the boxer Brian London's club. We were all meant to be back at the hotel and in our beds for about half past ten, but George and I rolled in about two o'clock.

The only thing for it at that unearthly hour was to try and tiptoe in through the emergency entrance and up the fire stairs. We thought we were like a couple of spies evading enemy capture and were just starting to congratulate ourselves on mission accomplished when we got to the top of the landing and found George Swindin sitting there waiting for us with his arms folded and a face not to be messed with. We got hell for that stunt! It was different in those days though; we didn't get fined because we weren't getting paid enough to start deducting money from our wages – there would have been uproar among the players had they tried to hit us in the pocket. Despite us breaking the curfew, George still picked me for the game against Burnley and I got a couple of goals, so I think he forgave me. I think he had a good idea of what I was like and how to handle me; I may have been bit of a joker off the pitch, but as soon as I got a shirt on and crossed that line I would get on with the serious business of playing for my team and make sure I gave it everything I had. The discipline at Arsenal was generally good, though. The club had been built on that kind of reputation and sometimes the approach was almost military. Ron Greenwood was certainly happy to have it that way, and wasn't really one for a laugh and a joke.

George Eastham has gone down in football history as the man who helped change the wage structure for players forever. He started the Professional Football Association (PFA) dispute when he came down from Newcastle, but it was Jimmy Hill who carried on with it and helped create the first £100-a-week player.

Like the rest of us, George had been on a maximum wage of twenty quid a week at Newcastle, less tax and rent, but when he challenged the money he was getting, he ended up in a bitter dispute with the club. At the time, clubs were able to hide behind a 'retain and transfer' system which gave them the right to hold on to a player's registration and refuse to pay them if they asked for a move. So when his contract ran out in 1959 and he told them he wanted more money or a move, they told him where to go. In the end, he told them: 'Pay me more or I'm not playing for you anymore.' They must have thought he was bluffing, but he was a strong-minded character and he stuck to his principles and went on strike for months. He walked away all right – he got a job instead selling cork for a mate of his dad's, keeping himself fit while he was frozen out of football. Amazingly, he was getting a tenner more doing that than he was playing in the First Division with Newcastle. Can you imagine that now – a cork salesman getting 50 per cent more than Michael Owen?

Anyway, the PFA took up his fight because he couldn't play for anyone else thanks to his contract with Newcastle, and it went all the way to the High Court. Newcastle backed off and let him join Arsenal for £47,500, but George wasn't prepared to let it drop and his fight against the injustice rumbled on for another three years, backed all the way by the PFA.

The way the PFA saw it, they could use George's battle as a test case, arguing that the transfer system was an unfair restraint of trade. It was a big gamble, because if the court had ruled against them I think it would have ruined them financially, as they would have been left to pick up an enormous bill for legal costs. But fortunately the judge saw it the players' way when he made his judgment in 1963. He booted the maximum wage into touch and opened up a whole load of new possibilities for players. This basically took away power from the clubs and gave it to the players, with the tribunal system set up to deal with cases where no agreement could be reached. I don't think you would have ever seen players like Michael Ballack and Andriy Shevchenko coming to Chelsea for twenty quid a week somehow. It was a landmark ruling back then, and the effects of it have shaped the way the game is run today, although there were never anything like the obscene amounts of cash there are now and a bit of realism on both sides – among players and directors, all we wanted was our fair share.

It was a personal triumph for George and great news for footballers everywhere. George made his Arsenal debut against

Bolton in December 1960, desperate to make up for lost time after his year in the wilderness. He was a joy to play alongside, and I remember him providing some great passes for me to feed off. We didn't really get too much abuse from opposition fans in those days; well, we did get some but we either laughed it off or did our best to ignore it. But I remember George getting a real hard time from the Geordies when we went up to play Newcastle. Typical of him though, he just channelled all the abuse positively, scoring to save us a point at St James's Park. He went on to become a bit of an Arsenal legend, even though he didn't play during a time full of trophies or success at the club, and he was also in Alf Ramsey's England squad for the 1966 World Cup – although he wasn't used.

Ipswich Town were the surprise winners of the league in the 1961/62 season, mainly due to the stream of goals from their forward Ray Crawford, but I wouldn't even make it till the end of the season with Arsenal. The board were starting to lose patience with my injuries and already they were putting the feelers out to see if they could claw back any of the money they had forked out on me in the first place. The hangover from the previous season showed no signs of clearing and we gave the supporters absolutely no encouragement that we were ready to put all the mediocrity behind us, winning just two of our first ten league games, and losing again to Spurs, this time 4-3 at White Hart Lane. There was a final highlight for me in an Arsenal shirt though, when I managed my one and only hat-trick for the club, banging in all three against Bradford City at Highbury as we finally managed to win an FA Cup game.

I didn't know it at the time, but it would be one of my last games for Arsenal. At least I had managed to score a hat-trick and I was pretty chuffed with that after fluffing the chance against

Everton the previous season when I took such a rotten penalty. The FA Cup hopes didn't last long though and this time it was Manchester United who knocked us out, 1-0 at Old Trafford. Arsenal would go on to finish tenth that season, but by then I was off, trying my best to get my career back on the road with Cardiff.

CHAPTER 14
STARS IN MY EYES

'I had no problem getting along with the rich and famous people
I met in London, and that meant there was never any shortage
of invites to parties, premieres and shows.'
MEL CHARLES

MOVING TO LONDON WAS A BIG culture shock for me, having come from a tight-knit community like Swansea, but being an Arsenal player opened a lot of doors and I soon found I was moving in highbrow circles with actors, singers, comedians and sportsmen. Arsenal were a glamour club, and because there had been a lot of publicity surrounding my transfer, and being John's brother, I was quite well known. I wasn't exactly an A-list celebrity, but it helped my social life enormously that I had a good sense of humour and had always been an outgoing chap. I had absolutely no problem getting along with a lot of the rich and famous people I would meet during my stay in London, and that meant there was never any shortage of invites to parties, premieres and shows.

Being injured a lot of the time was frustrating, and I could never shake off the sinking feeling that I was not living up to my potential. The papers would always be round the house taking pictures of me recuperating, sometimes with my slippers on and my foot on a stool as I tried to rest my damaged knee. In a couple of them I was pictured with my faithful dog Twinkle, who had gone with me from Swansea to London when I made the move to Arsenal. He was only a tiny thing, a little Maltese terrier, but he was a lovely dog. I had a boxer before that when I played for Swansea. I called him Nero – so you could say my taste in dogs went from one extreme to the other. Sitting around the house resting didn't do me much good though, and if I had the chance to be out and about doing something, then I would jump at it.

At times I could get quite down, but the friends that I made helped lift my spirits and I found the lifestyle a pleasant release. I got heavily into the showbiz side of London – I suppose the showbiz friends found me. They were such a friendly bunch, and because I was a sociable chap and enjoyed a night out and a bit of entertainment I was the perfect Arsenal player for them to befriend. I wasn't complaining; I loved every minute of it. The singers and actors appreciated us because we were footballers as much as we enjoyed hanging around with them. The press photographers weren't complaining either. It was hardly like the paparazzi that you see stalking celebrities now, but if they saw you out and about in the West End they would take your picture, and most of the time you didn't have any objection. It was nice to be noticed and to be seen out in the company of some of the big noises in London.

Bernard Breslaw, who is probably best known from the *Carry On* films, was my biggest mate. He used to have one of those big square Zephyr cars, and every Saturday when we were playing at

Highbury he would come round to the house and pick me up in his motor to take me to the ground. He was 6ft 7in and used to tower way above me. When the two of us knocked around together we must have looked like a pair of giants. He had this massive red-and-white knitted scarf that was wrapped all the way round his body – he made quite a sight! A fanatic Arsenal fan, he took a real interest in all our matches. I know some celebrities are accused of supporting football teams on a whim, and are seen by some supporters as hangers-on or glory-hunters, but Bernard could never have been accused of that. He was a regular fixture in the stand at Highbury for many years after I'd been and gone, and had a good knowledge of the game. Me and the wife used to go to all his shows. He would crack me up at times with his jokes and we got on like a house on fire. His wife Liz was a tiller girl and often we would go down to the West End as a foursome together. He had already been in a couple of films by that time, but he didn't really get his big break until the *Carry On* films… he used to have me falling about laughing when I saw him towering over little Barbara Windsor. What a pair they were, if you'll pardon the pun. Bernard deserved all the success he had because he was a fantastic bloke.

A regular highlight for me was the Sunday celebrity football matches they held for charity every couple of weeks round the various parks in London. As an Arsenal player I was obviously not allowed to join in, and the way my luck was going I probably would have got injured anyway, but they used to rope me in as the referee, because I was seen as a big name. That was a weird experience, because while I never had any real problem with refs during my time as a player, and never gave them any back-chat, I never harboured any ambition to be one and have a whistle in my mouth. It was all just a bit of fun though, and there was always a bit of banter flying back and forward between me and the players.

The showbiz XI included people like Bernard, and Mike and Bernie Winters, Dave King, Roy Castle and Dick Richardson, the boxer. We used to have marvellous times with a bit of a booze-up afterwards. Shirley Bassey would come along to kick off the match, and sometimes Petula Clark too. Shirley was a Cardiff girl and we always got on very well; she was great fun. We would bump into each other from time to time even after I had left Arsenal and London, and she even popped round my house in Cwmbwrla for a cup of tea and a drink in the local pub.

Another big mate of mine was the Irish actor Richard Harris – what a character! He absolutely loved the women, and I think they loved him back quite a bit too! They used to be falling over when they saw him sometimes. Richard used to take me and Mel Hopkins everywhere with him and he invited us as special guests to the premiere of the big war blockbuster he was in, *The Guns of Navarone*, in which he starred alongside guys like Gregory Peck and David Niven. It was great getting the red carpet treatment and seeing all the flashbulbs go off. We were all roughly the same age and on the same wavelength and we had some great times together. Richard was just starting out as an actor then, but you could see the potential he had, and after he was in *This Sporting Life*, playing a Rugby League star, his career went into orbit.

I was also pals with the painter Andrew Vicari from Neath, who is now mega-rich and famous. He was a struggling artist in those days, studying at the Slade School of Fine Art, and didn't have two pennies to rub together, so I helped him out. My wife and I used to invite him round to the house for Sunday dinner and we were quite good mates. Andrew knew all the same actors and singers that I was friendly with and made himself a few bob painting their portraits. I remember he painted a wonderful version of The Last Supper, with Richard Harris in it and me as Judas Iscariot! I think he made a few quid out of selling that picture, and eventually he became a world-famous artist. He's now based in Monte Carlo, but comes back to Wales from time to time. I've tried to get in touch with him in the past, but it's never come to anything.

When I was in London, I would meet up with my pals over at Tottenham from time to time – Cliffy Jones, Terry Medwin and Mel Hopkins – and go out for a meal or a drink with them, while I would tend to socialise mainly with Jack Kelsey and George Eastham at Arsenal.

While we were not exactly bosom buddies, me and Kelsey got on pretty well and had a few laughs together. We knew one another from the international matches and thought we might as well stick together as Welshmen at Arsenal. There was one time when our fellow countryman Brian Curvis, the boxer, came up to train with us both. He was one of the best boxers Wales has ever produced and what's more, he was Swansea born and bred. Brian was a welterweight and was training for British and Commonwealth title fights at the time and decided it would help his training regime if he did a bit of work with me and Kelsey. Neither of us would ever have claimed to have been the keenest or most dedicated of trainers in the squad – Ron Greenwood would certainly not have said so – and I think Kelsey could smoke about 300 fags in a weekend, but Brian was running backwards faster than me and Jack could run forwards. As fit as a fiddle, he was putting our fitness as footballers to shame. It was amazing the stamina and speed that he had and I suppose most top-drawer boxers are the same.

Brian kept on winning and eventually got a world title shot against Emile Griffith from the US Virgin Islands at the Empire

Pool. But Emile hit the hell out of him when they got it on in the ring. It was an amazing fight, but not for Brian; he was spitting blood for the next fortnight. It was quite a brutal bout too and went the full 15 rounds, because every time Griffith put Brian down he was back on his feet for more. I followed boxing quite a lot in those days and went to a lot of the big fights in London at Earl's Court, Wembley and so on.

Dick Richardson was another boxer we would knock about with from time to time. A heavyweight and a giant of a man, he'd been an army champion. He was hard as nails and did really well in his professional career. We went to see a couple of his big title fights, at the Empire Pool and Haringey Arena.

The pals I had from the world of entertainment and sport made sure I was able to stay happy-go-lucky. Life was good and while I would have given anything to be on the pitch playing every week instead of sitting on a treatment table having my knee tortured, I had enough going on with my showbiz mates to keep a smile on my face.

I never ever got ideas above my station though, and still saw myself as a man of the people. All the celebrities I mixed with had no snootiness about them anyway; they were just good, down-to-earth people who happened to have a talent and had gained a bit of fame because of it. Meanwhile I was still just the same working-class guy from Cwmbwrla and I never forgot it. I got on well with the Arsenal supporters in general and if they stopped me in the street for a chat or to say to hello, I would always make time for them. I was proud of my background and I enjoyed chatting to the fans and I think they in turn saw me as one of their own.

Being the biggest signing in Britain did have its advantages though and there were a few commercial opportunities that fell into my lap. I was always getting asked to advertise this and that, and I got a few bob extra pocket money for the privilege. The funniest advertising campaign I got myself involved in was a double act with Jimmy Hill. We had been hired to promote electric razors and it was one of the first adverts to go out on television. I think they approached me because I had been a big signing, while they no doubt picked Jimmy for the more obvious reason that he had the most famous chin in football.

We arrived at the studio to shoot the advert and they handed us the electric razors to get rid of the stubble we had sprouted for the occasion, but when it came to running them over our chin they wouldn't shift anything. Me and Jimmy were giggling away, it was hilarious. They must have been the first electric shavers invented, but there was clearly room for improvement – by about 100 per cent, because nothing came off! The advertising people flew into a panic and they had to quickly find some open razors so we could go away and have a proper shave. After doing it the old-fashioned way, Jimmy and I returned with skin like a baby's bottom and had to go on in front of the camera and say what a lovely shave we had just had with these fantastic new electric razors. They did manage to get better over the years as technology progressed, but I would never trust one of those things after that and I still use an old-fashioned razor to this day!

CHAPTER 16

A FANTASTIC FOUR

CHAPTER 15

A FANTASTIC FOUR

*'John Charles, who watched the game from the trainers' bench,
must have been delighted with the personal triumph of Mel
Charles, who scored all four goals – his first hat-trick
in an international.'*
SOUTH WALES EVENING POST, 1962

IT WAS ROUND ABOUT THE TIME of my transfer from
Arsenal to Cardiff that I attained one of my proudest
achievements with Wales – scoring four goals in one game in a
home international against Northern Ireland on 11 April 1962.
For all John did in his career, and that included a hat-trick or two
in the red shirt of Wales, he never managed four in one game for
his country, and I enjoyed winding him up about that! It's always
nice to get one over on your big brother.

The odd thing about that game was that the match was meant
to be played at the Vetch Field, but it was switched to Ninian Park
in Cardiff at the last minute because of a chickenpox epidemic in

Swansea. It was a real shame, because the town hadn't staged an international for 10 years, when Wales had beaten Northern Ireland 2-0 at the Vetch, and to miss out in circumstances like that was a real sickener – especially as Swansea's loss was Cardiff's gain. They even had the match programmes all printed up, with the Swansea Town chairman Philip Holden enthusing: 'For a town and district which have produced some of the most notable international footballers over the last decade, it seems appropriate that the Swansea public should have the opportunity of viewing some of these players in action on behalf of their country. I can only say how delighted we are to have a representative match here again, and trust it will be the forerunner of others and we shall not have to wait a further ten years for the privilege of staging international football.'

Sadly for Mr Holden and Swansea they were denied their chance to stage the game, but the move to Ninian Park certainly did me no harm and I knocked spots off the Irish.

The Wales team had changed a lot since the World Cup in Sweden, and I was one of the last survivors from Sweden along with Jack Kelsey, Stuart Williams, Mel Hopkins and Cliff Jones. Younger players like Terry Hennessey of Birmingham, Mike England of Blackburn and Malcolm Lewis of Orient had come through the Under-23 ranks and the three of them now formed a brand new half-back line, while Len Allchurch had forced his way into the team on the wing and Mel Nurse was knocking on the door for a place too. John was still playing for Wales at that time, but like me he was nearer the end of his international career than the beginning. He wasn't stripped against Ireland on this occasion, as he was in the middle of flitting between Leeds and Roma, but he had a pitch-side seat to watch his brother's biggest goal haul.

Like Wales, the Irish team had changed a lot since the World Cup too, but the great Danny Blanchflower – one of the main men during Tottenham's glory years under Bill Nicholson – was still going strong as their skipper, and they also had my Arsenal friend Terry Neill in their ranks. He was a good lad, and eventually went on to manage Arsenal, winning the FA Cup with them when they beat Manchester United in 1979. He would also get my Wales shirt after that famous game at Ninian Park where I managed to score my fantastic four.

The *South Wales Evening Post* reporter, Bill Paton, seemed to be a bit of fan of mine and he often had kind words to say about me. He didn't let me down when he recorded the goals the next day under the headline FOUR GOAL MEL! He wrote: 'John Charles, who watched the game from the trainers' bench, must have been delighted with the personal triumph of Mel Charles, who scored all four goals – his first hat-trick in an international. Good goals they were – especially the header from a Vernon lob into the goalmouth in the 34th minute. The others came in the 15th, 62nd and 67th minute. The first followed a powerful drive by Len Allchurch which Charles finished off and then, after the interval, a long ball from Lucas saw the Cardiff City player volley into the net before Briggs had time to move. The Irish keeper was obviously deceived by the speed of the low drive that passed underneath his body for the final goal.'

But just to keep my feet on the ground and my head its usual size, he added: 'Charles also missed a couple of sitters'! Four goals, and he reckons I should have had six! I was absolutely chuffed after that game, and I remember wandering around on cloud nine during the game. After I got a couple I was conscious I was on a hat-trick and the adrenaline started to flow, and when the third goal went in the feeling of elation is hard to describe. When I scored the fourth, I thought I'd better pinch myself as it all seemed more like a dream than reality. To score a hat-trick in an international match is such an honour, but to score four was amazing for me – fantasy football, really. The lads were brilliant towards me after the game and were chuffed for me, their grins almost as wide as the one I had on my face. I remember them all grabbing hold of me, winding me up that none of them could get near the ball because of me shooting all the time, and then chucking me head first into the bath.

Only three players have ever scored four goals in a match for Wales – me, Johnny Price against Northern Ireland, and Ian Edwards of Chester City against Malta – and I am really proud of my achievement. Even Ian Rush never managed that!

That was a great result for us, but we often seemed to do well against the Irish. I never even got the match ball to keep; I think I was so excited by the four goals that I just forgot to ask for it. I swapped shirts with Terry Neill after the game, so I was left with nothing to show for my efforts except an Ireland shirt – which got the same treatment as Pelé's shirt in the Swansea Sunday pub leagues! You just didn't think about those things – I didn't realise how significant it was. We didn't really hold on to things like caps and shirts; often we just gave them away. Terry actually made a few quid out of that shirt years later when it was auctioned by Sotheby's. It had been estimated that it would fetch about £800, but I was petrified there would be no bidders and I would be left looking like a lemon. I would have died of embarrassment if it went for something like fifty quid. I didn't have the cash to bid for it myself. In the end though, I needn't have worried; it went for something like two grand to a private collector. I just hope he values it more than I did at the time!

During that time I enjoyed a few more shenanigans with Wales.

While life was a bit of a rollercoaster at Arsenal, it was nothing compared to the real-life tremors witnessed in Mexico when I was over there with the national team. Mexico and Brazil invited us to play friendlies, so we went away on a tour after the summer of 1962 as a result of the friendships we had established with two of our opponents at the 1958 World Cup. I had done well against Pelé and co. in Sweden, but I couldn't pretend that I got near them the second time around. We had come so close to beating them in Gothenburg, and more or less matched them all the way, but they were streets ahead of us when they played us on their own patch. They were using the games as warm-ups for their defence of the World Cup in Chile weeks later, and they were taking the matches deadly seriously as they fine-tuned their game for the finals. They would go on to win it again too, with Pelé, Garrincha and Vava still firing in the goals for them. They were in top form against us and Pelé scored a hat-trick in the Maracana as they beat us 3-1 in front of more than 100,000 fans. They repeated the scoreline four days later in the second match in Sao Paulo.

Jack Kelsey got a bad injury in a 50/50 collision and he struggled for the rest of the tour, while I found myself in Jimmy Murphy's bad books for breaking a curfew and the code of discipline he had laid down. I felt really bad about that. I had travelled halfway across the world to represent Wales and I had blown it, but once you got on the wrong side of Jimmy Murphy you just had to take your punishment like a man, and I knew he was in the right to drop me.

We moved on to Mexico next, where the earth literally moved for us. While we were all relaxing in our hotel one day, the whole building started to shake – we were slap bang in the middle of a mini-earthquake in Mexico City and we found ourselves in a blind panic when the tremors started. We'd been warned beforehand that the tremors were not unusual and had been well briefed on all the emergency procedures in place, but I don't think you really take it all in. You're just saying to yourself, 'Yeah, yeah' and thinking it will never happen to you. The hotel had a big gap outside so if there's a tremor it's on an axle; I had never seen anything like it, but I knew that they hadn't put all those safety measures in place for the sheer hell of it and there was probably a real chance that something might happen. There were instructions on the bedroom wall telling you not to bother hanging about to get dressed or gathering together your belongings, just get yourself out of the building pronto and into the middle of the road. We were all in the hotel when it happened, and a panic-stricken Cliffy had obviously been reading the instructions because he ran out into the street at full speed wearing nothing but his underpants, and we weren't far behind him – heading for the middle of the road in terror and as far away from the building as possible like we'd been told. Dave Hollins, the goalkeeper, came running out with his two suitcases, trying to save all his wordly possessions, also wearing just his underpants. We must have been some sight, a squad full of internationals white as sheets and saying our prayers, huddled together in the middle of a street in Mexico City! All the bravado was gone, we were shit scared and there was no denying it.

Mexico was a lovely place, even in 1962, but some of the poverty left you down-hearted and feeling sorry for the people, those who had nothing. They were warm people and we had a lovely time walking round and taking in some of the sights. We must have stood out like a sore thumb because all the hawkers would start following us about and trying to flog us their gold chains and rings. Cliffy fell for their sales patter hook, line and sinker and ended up buying a gold ring, but it turned his finger green. One of the other lads bought a pearl ring for his missus, but the pearl fell out, so John got a bit of jam from the breakfast table and stuck it back in. All top-quality stuff!

The game was a bit of a terrifying experience, too. We were playing at an altitude of 7,000 feet, and although you could say Wales is a mountainous country, our hills were like pimples compared to the ones they had in Mexico. The air was so thin that you felt like you were gasping for breath most of the time, and that's before you even started running about and trying to play football. That wasn't a problem for me – Jimmy Murphy had stuck me on the subs' bench because I had gone AWOL for a few days on the Brazil trip, breaking all kinds of curfews, and was being punished for that. No excuses, just one of those crazy moments where you don't think things through. To rub it in, Jimmy handed me a green reserve goalkeeper's shirt, so there was me sat on the bench looking a complete wally in a green goalie's top.

There was big crowd for that game, about 70,000 I think, but we lost 2-1. All my team-mates were struggling out on the pitch and finding the high altitude unbearable. It was so hot you could hardly breathe – Cliffy Jones, Terry Medwin, they both went down like flies, and a few others were not far behind them. I had never been a goalkeeper, so I said to the manager for a laugh: 'Hey Jim, when do I get on?', but Jimmy just fixed me a cold look and said: 'When the goalkeeper fucking falls over, that's when YOU get on!'

John scored for Wales in that game but Antonio Jasso scored two for Mexico. He was their inside-left and a good player, but he was a bit of a firebrand and he ended up getting sent off along with Cliffy when they had a bit of a dust-up in the last couple of minutes. It was a real shame because Cliffy was normally a stickler for discipline and proud of his record, but he just got pushed too far, a bit like John had been during the Battle of Wrexham all those years before. Despite letting myself down with my own lack of discipline, it had been a good tour though and it was another fabulous experience seeing Mexico and Brazil, faraway places I could only have dreamed of visiting when I was a kid in Cwmbwrla.

While our adversaries from Gothenburg, Brazil, went on to enjoy glory again at the 1962 World Cup, we missed out and were unable to join them at the finals, because we had the misfortune to come up against Spain in the qualifiers. There wasn't a group stage in qualifying this time, just a straight knock-out, and sadly we came out second best. After experiencing the magic of the finals in Sweden it was a massive disappointment to miss out on the chance to do the same in Chile four years later.

We lost the first match 2-1 at Ninian Park, with Phil Woosnam scoring for Wales, and although we showed typical tenacity in Madrid a month later to draw 1-1, with Ivor Allchurch scoring our goal, we were out.

They had a fantastic side though, including the great Alfredo Di Stefano. He shouldn't even have been playing for Spain, but in those days the rules could be bent in exceptional circumstances where a player could represent more than one country. Di Stefano had started off playing for his native Argentina and scored five goals in six games, but when they made him a Spanish citizen he was allowed to represent his adopted country too. Puskas did the same when he stopped playing for Hungary and while he never came up against us, they had another guy, Feliciano Rivilla, in their team against us who originally played for Paraguay. The Spaniards had a habit of manipulating the rules to get the best players in the world in their side. Di Stefano's inclusion in the side is not sour grapes though, because they had a lot of other great footballers in their ranks, most of them on the books of Barcelona and Real Madrid, as you would expect. The brilliant outside-left Gento of Real Madrid was a joy to watch, and they reckon he was about the only winger in the world who could rival Cliff Jones for pace, while his club team-mate Santamaria was a rock at centre-half. They also had the Barcelona pair Gensana and Luis Suarez and you could only marvel at their ability. It says a lot for us that we came so close to beating them though and after drawing with them in Madrid, we could at least hold our heads up high despite the disappointment of missing out on a return to the World Cup finals.

My international career was starting to grind to a halt. I was picked to play for Wales against Scotland at Hampden in a game we lost 2-0, with a young Jim Baxter and Paddy Crerand pulling the strings for the Scots, although it was Ian St John who scored both the goals. I played against Scotland again at Ninian Park in Cardiff in 1962, but we lost that 3-2, with John scoring an absolute belter of a header, and my final appearance came the next year, in a 1-1 draw with Hungary at Ninian Park in one of the first European Nations Cup matches. That was a forerunner to the European Championships that we know now, and most countries used it to warm up for the World Cup qualifiers. Although I hadn't been involved, we had lost the first leg against Hungary 3-1 in Budapest the previous year. Because it was a knock-out format, and we were unable to overturn the deficit on home turf, we were dumped out in the first round. I didn't know it at the time, but that was to be my 31st and last appearance for my country.

CHAPTER 16
INTO THE BLUEBIRDS' NEST

'When I signed for Cardiff there was pressure on me immediately. They were up to their necks in relegation trouble and signing me was a last throw of the dice.'
MEL CHARLES

My knee was continuing to cause me problems at Arsenal, and by the time I found myself being edged towards the exit door at Highbury I had gone under the knife three times. I didn't do too badly, mind you, and had scored about 30 goals in 65 games – not a bad return for a team that was never really firing on all cylinders. But, if I'm being honest, I never really hit peak form at Highbury and with Tottenham doing so well, the pressure was on Arsenal to bring in new faces and freshen up the squad, and so I was put up for sale.

While I would have gone back to the Swans in a flash, they were very much a selling club, not a buying club and it was never really on the cards. When Cardiff City showed an interest it was the next best thing – a chance for me to go home to Wales.

The Bluebirds paid Arsenal £28,500 for me in February 1962, and to be fair to the Cardiff fans they were marvellous towards me. Although there has always been a fierce rivalry between Swansea and Cardiff, more so now than ever before, the fact that I had once played for Swansea wasn't an issue. The Cardiff supporters were just happy to see you trying to do your best for their club. A player's past didn't really enter into the equation.

Although Bill Jones was the Cardiff manager who actually signed me, ironically my manager at Arsenal, George Swindin, soon followed me to Ninian Park. He too hadn't lived up to the high – perhaps unfair – expectations in London, and tried to get his career back on track at Cardiff after a brief spell in charge at Norwich. Although he had bought and then sold me, we got on well and he was a manager I liked and respected. He also signed John, who by that time had moved from Juventus to Roma, and we got a brief taste of playing club football alongside one another for the first time. I settled in quickly at Cardiff, a club I liked, and by the end of my time there I had scored 25 goals in 81 league games.

You don't see it often now with the present-day Swansea and Cardiff sides but a lot of the time we were able to field an all-Welsh line-up. In fact, our fixture against Southampton on Hallowe'en 1962 at the Dell was the last-time for 40-odd years that Cardiff were able to name an all-Welsh line-up. The team was Graham Vearnecombe, Ron Stitfall, Trevor Edwards, Alan Harrington, Mel Charles, Colin Baker, Alan McIntosh, Alan Durban, Derek Tapscott, Ivor Allchurch and Barry Hole. We won that one 5-2 as well, which shows you what an all-Welsh side can achieve.

When I signed for Cardiff towards the end of the 1961/62 season there was pressure on me immediately. They were up to their necks in relegation trouble and signing me was seen as a last throw of the dice. They thought getting an established big-name international in might just do the trick and help them beat the drop. I was well used to pressure having been at Arsenal with that big price-tag hanging round my neck like a millstone, and here I was again going to a club where a lot was expected of me. Talk about jumping from the frying pan into the fire. I wasn't complaining though, I was just happy to be coming home to Wales.

My first match for Cardiff was a home game against Manchester City, and there was a big crowd of around 20,000 at Ninian Park willing me to mark my debut with a goal. I should have sent them home happy too, but I missed an absolute sitter. I think the club had some kind of relegation curse on them by then because nothing seemed to be going right for us. We drew that game against City 0-0, but worse was to follow the next week when we got a real going over at West Brom, losing 5-1. Confidence was low in the team, despite us having players like Barry Hole and Derek Tapscott, and we just couldn't stop sliding towards the trapdoor.

I bagged my first Cardiff goal in the next home game, a 1-1 draw against Burnley, and then came the game I was really looking forward to – Arsenal at Highbury, where I would be facing my team-mates of just a few weeks earlier. I was so desperate to get on the scoresheet in that match, but try as I might, I just couldn't find a way to goal. We did manage to pick up a point though in another 1-1 draw, but that was to be our last for a while because we went on an absolutely horrendous run, losing our next five and failing to score a goal in the first four of those defeats.

We had a couple of home games coming up and they represented a chance to try and wriggle our way towards safety.

We won them both – Tappy scoring a hat-trick against Birmingham and then another as we beat West Ham, but the final nail in our coffin was an 8-3 whipping up at Everton. The writing was on the wall – Cardiff were going down to the Second Division. I did manage to have the distinction of being the man to score Cardiff's last goal in top-flight football, as they haven't quite managed to get back up since. It came in our final game of that season, a 2-2 draw at home to Aston Villa. Good for pub trivia I suppose, but not much consolation for the poor Cardiff fans!

To be fair to the Cardiff board, they didn't take the relegation lying down. They were determined to try and bounce back quickly and win promotion to the First Division, and they showed their ambition by marking the beginning of the new season with another big-name signing – the Golden Boy of Welsh football, Ivor Allchurch. He made his debut in the curtain-raiser of the 1962/63 season, a rousing 4-4 draw with his old team Newcastle United at Ninian Park. The crowd of over 27,000 showed that the fans were willing to stand by the team too, despite the bitter disappointment of going down. I managed a goal in that game, but although I started that season as centre-forward, I soon found myself getting shifted around again, and there were a few weeks that I'd be played as a centre-half instead.

Cardiff had some good players in their squad. Bill Jones signed Peter Hooper from Bristol Rovers for £10,000 and he banged in 22 goals that season. He had a cracking left foot. I think Bill had promised him the same wages as Ivor and me if he did well, but that promise ended up counting for nothing when the manager lost his job not long after signing him and Peter ended up going back to Bristol, this time to play for City.

Quite early in the season I found myself back at the Vetch as Cardiff faced Swansea in the league in a midweek match. It was a very strange feeling as a Swansea lad and ex-player going back to face the Swans – especially in the blue and white of their arch-rivals. There was a big crowd crammed on to the North Bank, and although I scored for Cardiff that night, I think by and large the Swansea supporters were very warm and generous towards me and Ivor. They could afford to be too, because they won the game 2–1.

The fixture list in those days could be a bit chaotic and even though you had just played a team one week, you could find yourself facing the same opponents a couple of weeks later. And that was the case for the two South Wales derbies that season. The game at the Vetch had been on 4 September and the rematch at Ninian Park was on the 15th. A week is a long time in football, as the cliché goes, and the defeat at the Vetch proved one too many for manager Bill Jones, who didn't even make it to the second derby. Because we'd made a bad start to the season, and lost to our rivals Swansea, the board pressed the panic button and sacked him on 10 September – poor Bill was the first Cardiff manager ever to be sacked.

Our coach, Ernie Curtis, and one of the players, Ron Stitfall, took the team while the board scratched around looking for a new manager, but the two of them did a pretty good job and steadied the ship during a turbulent time for Cardiff. They got off to the best possible start. The Swansea fans didn't get to hold on to the bragging rights they had earned after their team's win at the Vetch for long, because without a permanent manager Cardiff still beat the Swans 5–2 at Ninian Park, with me scoring two.

I don't think I celebrated the goals at all. You didn't really get too carried away when you scored in those days anyway, but putting the ball into the Swansea net was not something I particularly enjoyed – you just had to be professional about it.

Cardiff City were paying my wages and that was the bottom line. I actually scored one of the best goals of my career in that game, too. I took the ball down on my chest at around the halfway line and went on a mazy dribble, beating four or five players before smashing the ball into the net, so to try and keep the celebrations low-key out of respect to Swansea was doubly hard. If it had been against any other team I would probably have gone on a lap of honour.

On 1 November, I had a sense of déjà vu when I found myself face to face with my new manager – George Swindin, my boss from Arsenal. We both had a laugh at the irony of it. Although he had bought me for Arsenal, he had also sold me, and now here we were again, thrown together by the football fates. Despite George coming in, it was still a bit of a mixed bag that season, though, and for every good result – most of them at home – there seemed to be a setback to keep us anchored in mid-table. We got walloped 6-0 at Chelsea, who were on their way back into the First Division, but beat them at Ninian Park, and that kind of summed us up. I remember it was a really bad winter, so a lot of games were called off during December, January and February, and we were left playing games every two or three days by the time the spring came. We were just inconsistent, plain and simple, and inconsistent teams can forget about entertaining thoughts of promotion. In the end, we finished up tenth.

CHAPTER 17
TEAM CHARLES

*'The Charles brothers were finally going to line up in the same
club side – but although we had grown up dreaming of us
both running out to play for the Swans, instead we would
be shoulder by shoulder for Cardiff.'*
MEL CHARLES

Cardiff were starting to get a reputation for making at least one
major signing a season, and they got the biggest of them all when
John joined us from Roma for the 1963/64 season. It was not the
smoothest of transfers you've ever seen however, and there was a
bit of a rumpus about it.

It hadn't really worked out for John in his second spell at Leeds,
his star was starting to fade a little, and when he went back to
Roma it was more a lifestyle choice than anything. His wife,
Peggy, couldn't settle back in Leeds second time round and who
could blame her – *la dolce vita* in Italy or cold winters in
Yorkshire? A bit of a no-brainer, I suppose. So John upped sticks

again and headed back to Serie A with Roma. But like I said, he wasn't quite the world-class footballer he had been, and when it never worked out at Roma he decided it was time to head home – and by home, I mean Wales.

Cardiff had tried to sign him a few times during the Fifties, but he was doing so well at Leeds that they were never likely to let him go to another club in the Football League. Juventus, of course, was a different matter and when they came in with an offer Leeds couldn't refuse, nearly £70,000, he had to go. So when Cardiff heard rumblings from officials at Roma that John would jump at the chance of coming to Wales, they dived in there as quick as they could.

The Cardiff chairman was Ron Beecher, a butcher to trade, and he was the one that was driving the transfer, trying to get all the other directors to agree. They knew that John would put a few extra thousand on the gate overnight, and with Ivor and myself already in the side, we would have a few big reputations and a lot of experience to pit against other sides.

There were a couple of other clubs sniffing about John too, Huddersfield being one of them, and when Cardiff decided how much they could afford to make the transfer happen they agreed on a final offer of £22,500 to Roma, take it or leave it. Roma took it, but only after a lot of huffing and puffing and Italian machismo from their directors, and John was coming home.

The big problem was that our manager George Swindin was making no secret that he was against the move. He already felt that he had an ageing squad on his hands – Ivor was well into his thirties by then, I was 28, John was 32, and we had other old-stagers like Tappy, Ron Stitfall and Alan Harrington in the side. The way George saw it, £22,500 was a massive amount of cash to be spending on one player, and he too suspected that while

John would obviously do a job for us in the Second Division, he was no longer the player who carried all before him at Juve. George reckoned that kind of cash could have bought him four or five young up-and-coming players instead, enough to prop up his squad for a decent crack at promotion, and I think he was seething with resentment, feeling that the board were riding roughshod over him and buying John regardless of whether he liked it or not. Later in his career he said in an interview: 'Big John is a great player but I needed youngsters. I didn't want old Welsh internationals coming home to Cardiff to grass.' Cheers for that one, George – I take it I was included in that little swipe, even if I was still going strong as an international at the time!

While the directors wanted to keep bringing the big names to the club to try and generate some good, positive, headlines, George certainly had strong suspicions that John was no longer the player he once was and advised them against bringing him to the club. As is usually the case, though, the board got their way, and John was in the team.

The Charles brothers were finally going to line up in the same club side – but although we had grown up kicking a ball in Cwmbwrla Park, dreaming of us both running out to play for the Swans together, instead we would be shoulder by shoulder in the Cardiff side. It's funny the way things work out.

The board's ploy to generate some positive headlines was working, though, and it didn't take long for the Charles-mania to begin, and by that I mean John, not me – I was back in the big fellow's shadow again. He played his first game in a Cardiff shirt in a friendly at Bath, and scored an own goal, but that was just pre-season stuff, nothing serious, and he showed enough class before that unfortunate OG to reassure the directors their money had been well enough spent.

Ninian Park was buzzing for John's league debut – his first game for a Welsh club after all his travels – and he didn't disappoint them. He got himself a debut goal and what a goal it was – there are Cardiff fans that still talk about it now. We won a free-kick well inside our own half and John smacked it high and long towards the Norwich goal. I don't think he had meant it as a shot, but it started sailing closer and closer towards their goal, and because it was an indirect free-kick it wouldn't have counted anyhow. That was until it bounced in front of their keeper, hit him on the shoulder, and flew into the net. The place went barmy, the fans were running on the pitch, leaping about and trying to pat him on the back as if we had just won the FA Cup! That was the effect he had on them. Football fans always need something to believe in, and the arrival of John at least gave them hope that some special times might just be round the corner.

That goal, plus one from Ivor, helped us to a 3-1 win and the fans' faith in John soared further still when we followed up our opening-day victory with another show of fighting spirit a few days later in a midweek game at home to Manchester City. We were getting beat 2-0, as they were a good side, but Ivor got us back into the game, then John headed in a last-minute equaliser to ensure his Messiah status continued a bit longer. Cue more pitch invasions as everyone again got caught up in the feelgood factor sweeping Ninian Park.

I suppose the Cardiff fans must have been thinking that John would be their saviour and would quickly get them back into the First Division. His arrival certainly gave us hope in the dressing room too, even if George still had his misgivings, rightly as it turned out. The fans were marvellous towards us too. There was still intense rivalry between Cardiff and Swansea even in those days, especially among the supporters. But we were all right, they were absolutely smashing towards us – John, Ivor and myself, two of us former Swansea Town players and John with an obvious Swansea connection, having been born and bred there and a former member of the ground staff at the Vetch. The Cardiff fans were very good to us throughout our time at Ninian Park, although like most football fans they were no angels when it came to giving their arch-rivals dog's abuse. When you were playing against them as a Swan it was a totally different matter – that's just the way it was, you accepted it and got on with it, but I'm glad to say they never ever gave me a hard time about my past. They just accepted you were trying your best for their club and gave you a fair crack of the whip.

There was a good team spirit at Cardiff too, despite the fact we were under constant pressure to take the club back up to the top division. Peter Hooper was a big mate of mine during my time at Ninian Park. He was a good player and used to live next door to me, with Ivor a couple of doors away and John another couple of doors along, and Tapscott and Colin Baker never lived far away either. We all stayed together in a lovely place on the road to Caerphilly, and there was good social scene. We would be round each other's houses all the time, and there were three pubs nearby – just for a lemonade, of course!

Big John coming in was maybe something of a false dawn for the club though. We didn't sense it in those early summer weeks of the season, but it was going to be another very tough campaign for us, again plagued by that big problem for any aspiring football team – inconsistency. I got injured after scoring the winner in a game against Northampton and was out for a couple of months, which didn't help matters, but both John and I were fit and playing in the derby against Swansea at the Vetch later in the season, me at centre-forward and John at centre-half – not a good day for us as it turned out, as Swansea were comfortable 3-0 winners. Again, the fixture list had gone crazy, and although I was injured at the time I do remember us playing Preston North End at home on Boxing Day, then playing them at Deepdale two days later! We'd have been as well joining them on the bus up to Lancashire after the first game to keep costs down. Just to keep things neat and tidy they beat us 4-0 both times – an 8-0 aggregate in the space of two days. Thank God I wasn't involved in that little double-header – that put George in a hell of a mood. He was already starting to feel the pressure and I noticed he wasn't as relaxed as he had been when we were together at Arsenal. He knew his job was on the line to get Cardiff back into the First Division and it was all starting to come apart. I wasn't the only one injured and we were struggling some weeks to get eleven fit players out on the park. The festive double-header against Preston was a particularly depressing blow – Cardiff helped make their Christmas a very happy one, with four points for them gift-wrapped by their generous Welsh friends. Can you imagine the fans' and clubs' reaction now if they tried to pull that stunt of playing the same side twice in a couple of days? They would be calling for heads at the Football League.

Leeds beat us in the FA Cup that season, which was a painful one for John. He played at centre-forward in that game with me at centre-half, just another example of the positional chopping and changing that went on with us. I suppose we saw it as a compliment that we were considered versatile, and to be honest, all you really want is to know that you have a jersey and that you are playing. Not that it was a joy to be playing that season. The chairman Beecher died, George was going round with a haunted look on his face, and not long after Christmas, a 5-0 drubbing away at Portsmouth led a lot of us to wake up to the fact that we were not going up. For all the early-season promise, Cardiff and the Charles Brothers would not be making a triumphant return to the First Division.

The League and FA Cup might have proved bitter disappointments for us in 1963/64, but at least the Welsh Cup was to provide us with a pick-me-up. It proved to be a lucky cup run for me too and I felt I earned my winner's medal because I scored in five of the seven games that we played. After beating Ebbw Vale, Chester and Newport County we played Bangor City in the final. We lost the first leg on their ground 2-0, but I managed to grab the final goal in a 3-1 win in the return at Ninian Park and forced a play-off. They didn't bother with extra time in those days, and they just took the view that another fixture would not be any hardship for us. After all, we were being paid to play football, so go out and play football. You hear all the talk these days about too many fixtures and players getting tired, but in those days we would regularly be playing 50 or 60 games a season, not to mention friendlies that were also fixed up at a moment's notice. The play-off had to be held at a neutral venue, and they played it at the Racecourse Ground at Wrexham. We won 2-0, Peter King scoring them both, and John and I were cup winners together at last. It was a good feeling celebrating next to him in the dressing room and I think we caught each other's eye and didn't have to say anything – while the Welsh Cup was often billed as the 'poor relation' of the football season, it meant a lot to us and if you win any cup it should mean a lot to you. A lot of players go through their entire careers without winning a medal, and I was proud to get my hands on one after that win in Wrexham.

Sadly for George Swindin, he was sacked days before we won the Welsh Cup. I personally was sorry to see him go, he always played fair with me, and I think it was a bit of an impossible job he had on his hands. Poor George also missed out on a glamour tour of Italy, organised as part of John's transfer deal. We were going out there for three games – against John's former teams Juventus and Roma, and a lower-division team Latina – and in the absence of a manager, the trainer Ernie Curtis was in charge of the team.

Because I had been out to Italy in the past while John was at Juventus, I knew what a sensation he was over there, but the rest of the team were left absolutely gobsmacked by the reception he got. It was one thing being a hero in Britain – a few autographs here and there, maybe the odd advert or endorsement, but in Italy they treated their top footballers like Gods and worshipped the ground that they walked on. As soon as we arrived, John was showered with gifts. He was the interpreter for the whole party, and with typical modesty he did his best to play down all the accolades that were being rained down on him. We didn't need to understand Italian to work out just how much they loved him.

The first match of the tour was against Juventus, who used to play in a ground called the Stadio Communale, and their fans went wild at the mere sight of John and started chanting 'Charlo, Charlo!' That was my nickname too, and maybe it did the trick, because I gave Cardiff a surprise lead early in the game. Big John then made it 2-0, and again the shouts of 'Charlo, Charlo!' started echoing round the stadium. Even though it was only a friendly, the Italians never like losing and the fans' jovial mood quickly turned ugly when Ivor Allchurch made it 3-0 at half-time. The songs and merriment disappeared and Juventus were booed off the pitch as we headed into the dressing room scarcely able to believe we were running riot against one of the giant clubs in European football.

As we came out for the second half, I saw one of the most amazing sights I have ever witnessed at a football match. Like I mentioned, the hero worship Juventus and their fans reserved for John knew no boundaries, but the stunt they pulled off to show their gratitude was like something out of a James Bond film. A helicopter flew over the stadium and dropped a little parachute, which floated down towards the centre circle. We were falling all over each other to go and see what was attached and there was a hush of silence round the stadium as the fans waited to find out what was going on. Tied to the parachute was a little velvet cushion with a gold watch – served up in the ultimate style for John. They loved him in Turin, I'd never seen anything like it.

Maybe that distraction cost us a famous win though. Juventus had obviously got a rollicking at half-time for their dismal efforts in the first 25 minutes and they had been ordered to get out there and avoid an embarrassing defeat. They upped their game immediately and were a different side after the break, scoring three goals in the last 20 minutes to rescue a face-saving draw. With the Juve fans happy again, they streamed on to the pitch at the end and carried John off on their shoulders. There's no doubt we were just there to make up the numbers – the match was all about John and it was his big day. But they were marvellous towards the rest of us too, they really went out their way to make us feel welcome because we were the team that *Il Gigante Buono* now played for. He was mobbed everywhere he went in Turin, but he shook every hand and signed every autograph book that was thrust his way.

We were loving every moment of our Italian adventure and the hospitality was wonderful. There wasn't the pressure that you would later find in European competition – we were there to enjoy ourselves, try and enjoy our football, and make the most of a beautiful place. Maybe we were a little bit too relaxed by the time we played Roma in the second game, because they comfortably beat us 4-1. John was a big hit with their fans too, even though he hadn't had anywhere near the same impact at the club as he had done at Juventus. He was cheered and applauded every time he touched the ball, but Roma were well up for the game and deservedly brushed us aside. That probably knocked the confidence out of us a little, and when we lost the final game of the tour 4-3 to Latina, it was time to go home and start life under our new manager.

George Swindin – the man who had bought me, sold me, and then ended up with me in his side at Cardiff, was gone. He had been a familiar face for me and I enjoyed working with him, not really something I could say about his replacement Jimmy Scoular.

Scoular – my third manager at Cardiff in as many years – was a dour bugger and we never really saw eye to eye from the start. Jimmy wasn't a mixer socially, he was gruff and probably the complete opposite to me, which is no doubt the root cause of why we never got on. I remember we used to sometimes have bounce games at training, where the A team played against the B team, and while it was only really meant to be a training exercise, Jimmy saw it differently. While we would all be wearing training shoes, he would go out there and strap on these big boots with long studs and then try and kick the hell out of us all. Maybe he was just trying to toughen us up a bit, but we already knew how to handle ourselves, especially the more experienced members of the squad. No, more likely, it was because that is exactly the way he was as a player, he just wanted to show us he was the boss and not to mess with him.

He was a legend up in Newcastle during his playing days, one of those guys who would go through a brick wall if you asked him to do it. But while he was a cracking player and was capped by Scotland, he had a really nasty side to him too, and he enjoyed taking out an opponent every now and again. They called him the Iron Man and that was an accurate nickname for Jimmy. While I got the impression that he didn't have too much time for me, he was far more blatant in his dislike for Ivor Allchurch. I think he harboured a grudge because Ivor had gone to Newcastle and taken a bit of his glory away as a favourite of the fans. I think the two of them had quite a few run-ins during their time together at Newcastle, probably because they had such a contrasting approach to the game, and when Jimmy became Ivor's boss at Cardiff he let him know in no uncertain terms that he had a long memory. There was friction between the two of them from day one. I saw Scoular from time to time after I'd finished playing. He played in a lot of charity games and also played for the John Charles XI in Mauritius when I went out there, but I didn't hold any grudges. We just had two totally different personalities and it would have been a complete waste of time to pretend that we could get on well with each other. So, most of the time, we just kept our distance. He was one hard bastard, though!

It all came to a head between Jimmy and me the following season when I scored a hat-trick for Cardiff in a 3-3 draw away to Swindon Town, then found I'd been dropped for the next game a couple of days later. I marched straight to Jimmy's office and knocked on the door, demanding to know why I'd been left out – with good reason, I reckon. I mean, what manager would drop his striker the game after he scored a hat-trick? I was such a laid-back character it took a lot to get me riled, but I was close to a rage when I confronted him. He told me while he couldn't argue with the goals I had scored, in his opinion I hadn't worked

hard enough and done enough running off the ball for my team-
mates – something of a slap in the face after me banging in a hat-
trick! His office at Ninian Park overlooked a field with a couple
of mangy old horses in it, so I pointed to one of the horses and
told him: 'You could put a number eight shirt on him and he
would run about all day – but he wouldn't score a fucking hat-
trick for you!'

That was my last word, and my final game! He freed me from
my contract after that and I never played for Cardiff again. At least
I had gone out having scored three goals in my last game in a
Cardiff shirt.

What I did regret was missing out on a lot of the European
football that season. By winning the Welsh Cup we had qualified
for the European Cup-Winners' Cup, but my only taste of
European football with Cardiff was the away leg of our tie against
the Danish side Esbjerg. After I left, Cardiff managed to get past
them and then they also beat Sporting Lisbon, Tappy scoring the
winner in a famous victory in the Stadium of Light. He must
have been one of the shrewdest signings Cardiff ever made –
Tappy never gave defenders a moment's peace and always gave
everything in a game. They went and got a draw with Real
Zaragoza too, but were knocked out of the competition when
they lost the return at Ninian Park. But my days at Cardiff were
over. I was looking for a new, exciting challenge so I could start
enjoying football again, and amazingly it came in non-league
football, in the League of Wales.

CHAPTER 18

LAST PORTS OF CALL

'I had more money at Porthmadog than I did when I was playing for Arsenal. They treated me like a king and I started to really enjoy my football again.'
MEL CHARLES

I WAS DISAPPOINTED with the way it finished up for me at Cardiff, because I liked it there. They were a good club and I had got my appetite for football back during my return to Wales after the frustration I experienced at Arsenal. But in the grand scheme of things, leaving Ninian Park worked out well for me. Little did I know it when I started playing at Traech for Welsh League side Porthmadog, but I was about to embark on the most enjoyable time of my football career. The pressure was off, the fans were great, and I had an absolute ball. I wasn't doing it out of the goodness of my heart, if I'm being honest, because the club were being bankrolled by a millionaire and they were paying me well. Amazingly, I was earning more money in North Wales than I had been earning at Arsenal or Cardiff. The money was nice, but more importantly I had fallen in love with football again and they treated me like a king.

They were a proud club with a history stretching back to 1884, but when a holiday and caravans tycoon called Graham Bourne decided to plough some money into Porthmadog in 1965, he changed the way the club operated almost overnight. During that summer, he managed to persuade the committee that they should abandon their amateur policy and start trying to recruit some big-name players. Graham wanted to put the club on the map and have some fun doing it. He was absolutely loaded and it was his cash that helped to lure me to Porthmadog.

Bourne had opened a caravan park called Greenacres in Porthmadog and felt that he would be giving something back to the community by financially backing the town's football team. When he was able to deliver them success, I think he had succeeded in winning their hearts and minds, as he had set out to do, but he also enjoyed every minute of the football experience too. The club became more and more of a passion for him rather than just a plaything.

In my first season with the club, 1965-66, Porthmadog finished second behind Caernarfon Town in the Welsh League, but we won the Alves Cup, beating Rhyl in the final, and also got to the final of the Cookson Cup. Finishing runners-up in the league was just a curtain-raiser for the success that was to follow and for the next three seasons Porthmadog were unstoppable in our own league, winning the title each year. We had developed a winning mentality and we scored goals for fun. The style of football was all-out entertainment and the fans lapped it up. They had enjoyed something of a golden era a decade earlier, with a few cup wins to celebrate, and the fans really responded well when we started to sweep all before us in the late Sixties, and took especially well to me.

We used to have a following of 1,500 people wherever we went, because they loved their football up there in North Wales, they were fanatic about the game. We narrowly missed getting into the European Cup-Winners' Cup though, because I botched a bloody penalty in the Welsh Cup. It wasn't as bad as the daisy-cutter I took when I missed out on a hat-trick for Arsenal, but it personally proved to be as big a source of regret because I would have loved the chance to play in Europe for Porthmadog. We had some cracking players in the side, all dedicated guys who would sweat blood for the team. There were good local lads like Dave McCarter and Jo Williams, the goalkeeper was Ivor Pritchard, and throughout the team we had other seasoned players like Mick Porter, Gwynfor Jones who had played for Wolves, the former Sheffield Wednesday player Pat Laverty and my mate from Swansea and Wales, Des Palmer. I also managed to persuade Colin Webster to sign, and he scored a lot of goals in the two seasons he played, so for a Welsh League club we had a something of a star-studded side.

Coming from the Football League into the Welsh League, and a slower pace, was easy in a way. I think one or two opponents tried to single me out and attempted to make a name for themselves, but I did okay, I knew how to handle myself. Plenty of them tried to make their mark, literally on my legs at times, but I was still a little bit too crafty for some of them.

We got well used to winning, and while most of our success came in the league, there was one classic cup tie against Swansea in the Welsh Cup when 3,000 fans crammed into the Traech. We should have beaten them too, but drew 1-1 and were taken to a replay. A lot of the Welsh Cup games had to be played on midweek afternoons in those days, just to squeeze them into the fixture list, and for the replay the council were giving all the schools in the area a half day so the kids could join the exodus from Porthmadog to the Vetch. There was a crowd of nearly 11,000 for that game, Swansea's biggest of the season, but sadly we lost.

I think I enjoyed Porthmadog so much because when I was at Arsenal there had been so many rules and regulations. They always did things by the letter of the law and while I respected that it was their right to do so, this left me frustrated at times. I always remember the time when George Swindin called me to his office at Highbury. When I walked in he had such a stern look on his face that I knew I was in his bad books for something. As it turned out, I was being hauled over the coals for something quite innocent. I had been on my way home after training one boiling hot day, and I had just got off the Tube and I had to pass a pub at the end of my road to get to the house. I called in for a pint, just one shandy, but while I was there innocently sipping away I think eight people phoned the club saying they had seen Mel Charles drinking in the pub. They were all exaggerating the various states of drunkenness I was supposedly in. If the eight snitches were all to believed, I had sunk eight pints, when all I had was one bloody shandy! But George had to take all the calls, and he was only doing his job by calling me into his office and reading the riot act. Arsenal saw you as a professional footballer and that meant you shouldn't be drinking, and even though I protested my innocence, I'm not sure he believed me. That turned out to be an expensive shandy!

Porthmadog was completely different though, and I was allowed the run of the place. I was getting more than thirty quid a game because the chairman had so much money and he wasn't shy about dishing it out. Graham Bourne used to have caravan parks all round the coast and I would take the family up there in the summer. I didn't have to pay a penny, he insisted on taking care of everything, and I was very well looked after. I would always pop into the pubs up there too and got on brilliantly with the supporters and locals. It was just a magic time for the club and everyone walked around with a smile on their face. I had discovered a whole new world of football to which I had been oblivious before, and I loved every minute.

A lot of the supporters would wear badges with 'Our Mel' written on them, and that was the way they saw it – I was theirs.

But nothing lasts forever, and when the chance came along for one last crack at playing in the Football League, with Port Vale, I took it. One of their supporters, Rol Williams, even wrote a poem about me after I left – it was quite touching really. It went like this…

In eighteen months he scored some goals
And others he saved well
For in North Wales they all did fear
The power of our MEL

And as the high balls came across
'Right Ivor!' he did yell
For in command right through the game
Without a doubt was MEL

The story of 'That penalty'
Remains for some to tell,
But let us not forget, of course
No man is perfect MEL

But in his last game at the Traeth,
Revenge had such sweet smell
That goal from fully 40 yards
Was typical of MEL

His Wolseley 1500 car
Could not be classed as 'swell'
But from Cwmbwrla to the Traeth
It safely brought our MEL

The book is closed and we are told
Porthmadog had to sell
And at Port Vale we all do wish
The best of luck to MEL

Despondent let us never be
For you can never tell,
The Traeth at Port may give again
A welcome back to MEL

I had some absolutely fantastic times at Porthmadog, and I really enjoyed going back there a few years ago as their guest of honour. I shook hands with all the present players and was given some really warm hospitality. They remain a great little club to this day. Sadly for Graham Bourne, however, he died in his mid forties, but there's no doubt he brought some special memories to the club.

When I had signed for Porthmadog I thought I was finished with League football, but out of the blue a chance came up to play for Port Vale. One of the directors at Porthmadog had the opportunity to get on the board at Port Vale, but only on condition that he took me with him. Sir Stanley Matthews was the manager and we became great mates. A cracking man, his contribution to football has gone down in folklore. He did his best as manager at Port Vale, but the club was always up against it and we seemed forever to be taking one step forward and two steps back.

Stan was the first footballer to be knighted and when the trainer and caretaker manager at Port Vale, Jack Mudie, along with the director Arthur McPherson, managed to persuade him to make the switch from Stoke City to Port Vale it was seen as a big coup at the time. He was a Stoke legend so it was a big deal then for him to go to Port Vale, but he relished the challenge. It was Stan's first crack at management, and with the club toiling away in the Fourth Division, it was a measure of the man that he agreed to work for expenses only. You couldn't help but admire him.

Vale Park was a big cavern of a ground then, and the games were no place for the faint-hearted. It was good to meet up with George Eastham again, because he was playing just along the road with Stoke City, and I also got on well with their player Maurice Setters as well.

Coming out of the Welsh League and playing in the Fourth Division was bloody rough. There were some hard bastards in that league and they knocked me about a bit. I remember we played Crewe and Walsall and in both games their centre-halves clobbered me early in the match. I could hardly get up and by the end of the game I was struggling to walk off the pitch. I couldn't take much more of that, and although Port Vale wanted me to stay on, I had had enough of that. I think I'd got used to the Welsh League and the comfort of being the big fish in a little pond, and getting used as a punchbag in the Fourth Division didn't really appeal to me at that stage of my career.

Stan only lasted three years as manager of Port Vale and the club ended up in deep trouble soon after and were thrown out of the

Football League because their finances were a mess. They were a club living on past glories and were stuck in a rut. Although I enjoyed working alongside Sir Stan and we became really good friends for years to come, my brief spell with Port Vale was not one that I look back on with particular fondness.

I bailed out after just a handful of games and went back to the Welsh League, briefly with Oswestry Town, who have evolved over the years and are now better known as The New Saints, but it was at my next club, Haverfordwest County, where I was to have some more happy times as my career entered an Indian summer.

My knees were starting to really give me gyp and I was beginning to play more and more as a centre-half rather than a centre-forward. Like Cardiff, Haverfordwest are known as the Bluebirds, and they were a lovely little club. I was there nearly five years, played nearly 200 games, and I have nothing but wonderful memories. They are another club who have invited me back recently to meet their fans and players. It's a lovely feeling when you realise that you are still appreciated to this day and it can be quite emotional when they parade you on the pitch at half time. You also meet supporters who were around when you were playing, who refresh your memory with some of the good times you had together.

I would always make a point of going to socialise with the fans after a game – win, lose or draw – and I think they really appreciated that. I also remember playing Father Christmas at the kids' Christmas party, which went down well. I probably had the girth to play the role quite well by that time, mind you! I had lost a bit of my pace, and had put on a pound or two from the lean, mean physique I had earlier in my career, but my heading ability was still a useful weapon and the fans used to tell me that I could header a ball further than most players could kick it!

The players were all a smashing bunch, and they would give

their all. There was one game against Ton Pentre where George Brain went over badly on his ankle, because the pitch was full of pot-holes. I told him just to run it off, as that is what I would always try and do, and because he had just a good attitude to the game, that's exactly what he did. The only trouble was he had broken it – but after a quick dab of the sponge and a quick bandage up, he ran about the best he could for the rest of the game. That was the type of team spirit we had.

I was really enjoying my football, maybe sub-consciously aware that I didn't have too many years left in the tank, and I gave 100 per cent in every game. I remember we were playing a Swansea Town select side in a pre-season friendly behind closed doors at Clarbeston Road. The game was being refereed by a farmer, who is the father of Barry Vaughn, club secretary at Haverfordwest now. When I asked him how long there was left, he said there were just a couple of minutes to play. I was enjoying the game so much that I asked him if he could play on for another twenty minutes. He said, 'No, I have to get back and milk my cows'. I told him if he let us play on for another 20, I would come back to his farm and milk his cows for him. He couldn't help laughing, but he never did play any extra time. He should have done it just to see me making a prat of myself, trying to milk his cows. But he did pay me a big compliment after the game when he told me after the game that he couldn't believe that a man who had played for Arsenal, for Wales, and who had played in the World Cup finals, still had so much enthusiasm for the game that he wanted to carry on for an extra twnty minutes in what amounted to a meaningless game in a small town in Pembrokeshire.

We also had the evergreen Ivor Allchurch in our ranks, and while he too was coming to the end of his career, he was still a marvellous player. You just don't lose ability like that, and although his pace may have started to fade, he still had all the tricks and was a pleasure to play alongside. He remained the Golden Boy of Welsh football and he enjoyed his time at Haverfordwest so much that he went on to become player-manager there.

I didn't last as long as Ivor because my recurring knee problems were starting to make it impossible for me to keep playing at a decent level. There was no way I was ever going to turn my back on football completely though and I started running my own team in Swansea after my days at Haverfordwest. While I was still playing, I was probably doing my knees more damage every time I pulled the boots on. My team was called Cwmfelin, which was run out of a social club in Cwmbwrla. We played against the Swansea colts at St Helens and beat them to win the local cup. They've still got our photograph up in the club to this day. That was a great feeling because they had all the young professionals turning out for them. We also won a few championships, but it was just for fun by that stage. I had returned to playing centre-forward, as I was only interested in scoring goals by that stage and I think I got six or seven in one game.

I was well into my thirties by then, but I already had a bad leg and would be limping around for days after each game. I've now had kneecap replacements in both legs, and the left knee was the main problem. I remember going in to get the second one done at Morriston Hospital and the nurse asked me for an autograph while I was lying on the trolley, waiting to go to the operating theatre. I had to ask her twice 'I beg your pardon' because I was lying flat out on the trolley at the time and I thought she was having some kind of joke at my expense. I still signed it, mind you!

CHAPTER 19
MEAT AND METAL

*'After football, I pretty much tried everything. Nothing went right
for me because I wasn't business-minded. If it was a choice
between potatoes or paradise which one are you going to pick?'*
MEL CHARLES

YOU SEE THE MONEY that players are paid now, the advice
they get and how well they're looked after by their clubs and
agents, and it's a far cry from the world in which we operated in
as footballers in the Fifties and Sixties. We didn't have it easy after
we had retired either: we were on our own and left to make our
own stupid mistakes – and boy, did I make some!

In common with most players of that generation, I hadn't really
given much thought to my future beyond football and when I
was forced to quit the game I was virtually penniless, with not the
slightest idea of what I should do next. It started going through
my mind that maybe I should have stuck in at school a bit more
and paid more attention in lessons, but that feeling always passed

quickly enough because I wouldn't swap the life I had in football for anything. My lack of a good education and the fact that football was practically all I knew didn't exactly stand me in good stead for trying to make a living after I had retired though. I tried every bloody thing going, but each venture seemed to end in the same way – with me flat broke.

I worked briefly for my cousin and he sent me up to the valleys as a door-to-door salesman, trying to flog shoes and frocks, and so on. It sounded so easy, and it probably should have been, but I was such a sucker for a hard-luck story that I didn't have the temperament to be a salesman. I just wasn't cut out for it – I gave away half the stock I was meant to be selling and felt better for it. When I saw skinny little kids standing there with no shoes on their feet and not a penny between them, I took pity on them and gave away all my shoes. I must have thought I was Robin Hood or something, only I was taking from my cousin to give to the poor, and that wasn't the best idea if I was meant to be working for him. Some door-to-door salesman I was – half the time I didn't even make it as far as the door! My cousin was livid, as you might expect, when I returned with an empty suitcase and empty pockets too. He said I was going to bankrupt him if I kept doing my Mother Teresa act and in the end he suggested, as gently as he could, that maybe I should seek an alternative line of work. I took the hint.

From there I went into the scrap metal business with John and we based ourselves between Cardiff and Swansea. We bought a lorry and had a lot of good contacts, and it should, in theory at least, have been a big success. True to form, we didn't get very far. We were both too laid back to make a business work. I think one of us in charge of a business was bad enough, but when you put the two of us together, we had absolutely no chance. From the moment we set up business together, we were fighting a losing battle. Already we were starting to struggle to keep our heads above water with one thing or another when I made a fatal mistake. I got a phone call from the manager of a private yard, and he was keen to do us a favour and told me to bring the lorry up and take whatever scrap and steel I wanted. I took it a bit too far though, because I thought he had literally meant take ANYTHING.

I loaded up the lorry with all the scrap and steel I wanted, like he had said, but I took his bloody weigh bridge too. The lorry barely made it back to Swansea, as it was creaking under the weight. The manager bloke was straight on the phone to me, shouting and screaming, and asking what the hell I was playing at. He wasn't the least impressed when I reminded him that he had said I was welcome to take anything. The upshot was that he took me to court. The judge was a big rugby man and it was well known in town that he did not have any time for footballers. He had even less time for me when I blundered my way into court like Frank Spencer and addressed him as 'Your Highness'. I was just nervous and I reckon he was enjoying watching me squirm. He said to me: 'Mr Charles, would you kindly tell me what happened up there?' I said: 'Your Highness, the bloke told me to take all the steel and that's all I did.' With a sigh, he said: 'But you took the weigh bridge, Mr Charles' and when I replied: 'Well, that's steel, isn't it?' he was not impressed. He fined me, told me to get out of his court and never come back, and that was the end of the scrap metal business for me.

From my catastrophic dalliance in metal, I then tried meat, selling cooked chickens round the pubs. I would buy up big batches of around four dozen at a time and then drive round all the pubs and clubs selling them. They usually went down a storm and it seemed like a good number. I would go into a club called The Regency every Friday and the punters would be queuing up to buy the chickens from me, but by the time I got there on one particular Friday, I only had one left. A whole load of regulars were depending on their chickens to keep their wives happy, feed the family, whatever, and there was I, about to get lynched because I had turned up almost empty-handed. The only one that I had left was a scrawny little thing and everyone was screaming at me, 'Mel, where's my chicken?'

The bloke behind the bar had a brainwave and said: 'Why don't you raffle it, Mel?' It seemed like a good idea, and somehow we managed to sell a hundred-odd tickets for a chicken that none of the drinkers had even seen. The guy who won the raffle then found that his girlfriend had gone home with his ticket, so when the barman said no ticket, no chicken, we raffled it all over again. We'd taken in hundreds of pounds for this sorry-looking chicken and I had somehow managed to make a tidy few quid. The winner wasn't too impressed when he saw how little meat was on it and we all had a good chuckle at his expense. I didn't have a smile on my face for long though, because not long after that the council's environmental health department got on to me and put me out of business. They reckoned my car didn't comply with the strict hygiene standards they had in place for anyone selling meat and told me to get it sorted or seek alternative employment.

There must have been something about me and meat. Undeterred, I tried my hand at running a butcher's business. Sadly, that ended in chaos as well. The idea was spawned when I got talking to a master butcher who was a bit down on his luck and looking for work. I took pity on him and decided to let him run a shop for me, not far from my old house in Alice Street. It was the perfect spot for a butcher's and we quickly built up a steady stream of satisfied customers. The business was going really well and sometimes it would be queued out the door. The guy was great at his job and I thought I was on to a winner, but then I got an invite to go away for a couple of weeks to teach head tennis to some kids at a holiday camp in the Isle of Wight. My butcher was doing such a good job and business was booming so much, I thought nothing of leaving him in charge. After all, what could possibly go wrong? But when I phoned home, my father asked me what had happened to the shop – why was it closed, and why was there a pile of raw meat rotting away in the front window? Alarm bells started ringing immediately and I got myself back to Swansea pronto.

When I arrived at the shop to find out what the hell was going on, sure enough it was all locked up and my fly-by-night butcher had left. By the time I got back the meat in the window was crawling with bluebottles and I had one hell of a mess to sort out. It turned out he had buggered off with all the takings and just to rub salt into the wounds, he had gone round all the restaurants and hotels that we supplied and cleaned me out of all the cheques we were owed as well. He took the lot and I never saw or heard from him again. It was a real slap in the face considering I was only playing the Good Samaritan by helping him out in the first place.

If at first you don't succeed, try, try again, and that's what I did, this time throwing my lot in with the potato business. It started off well and I supplied most of the fish and chip shops in Swansea. Just like the butcher's shop I briefly kidded myself on that I had discovered a winning formula. Money was pouring in, we had no shortage of business, and again it looked like nothing could go wrong. But yet again, fate intervened, or in this particular case John did.

He was out on the island of Mauritius in the Indian Ocean with his select side, the John Charles Eleven, and they were playing a series of matches there. He gave me a call and said I should come out and join him. Ivor and Len Allchurch were there, along with Roy Saunders of Liverpool, Terry Medwin, Jimmy Scoular and the former Aston Villa keeper, Nigel Sims. It was an invitational side and John said he would love to see me out there. He was doing his best to sell the idea to me, saying it was one of the most beautiful places on earth, and that it would be like heaven to me. Although I was sorely tempted by his description, for once I did my best to play the serious businessman and said 'No John, I've got to stay here and look after my business.' John said: 'fair enough', but that I should at least take a look at the brochure he was going to send me before I made up my mind.

He sent me the pamphlet as he had promised and after I had taken one look at the bikini-clad girls on the front, sunbathing in an exotic paradise, I said to myself: 'That'll do me' and was on the first plane out there. I asked John how long it would be for and he told me a fortnight, so I thought, sod it, why not? I was only meant to go there for a couple of weeks, but I ended up staying for months and while the boss was away the potato business went down the pan. Mauritius looked like paradise in the pamphlet, and it was! I came back with a suntan and some brilliant memories, but with no business left. If it was a choice between potatoes or paradise, which one would you pick? I heard later that because of my little extended holiday in the sun, a lot of the fish and chip shops in Swansea had to shut down for a few days because they didn't have any potatoes! Their supplier had left them high and dry while he was out having himself the time of his life in Mauritius. After that, the chips were well and truly down for me. My reputation had gone, so there no more jobs for me to mess up.

Going to Mauritius had been a foolhardy thing to do, but it didn't seem like it at the time. I think we played about six matches out there with John's team, but there was plenty more to the trip than just football. When we went to Mauritius, Cliffy Jones wasn't able to make it and Roy Saunders filled in as my main sidekick. Roy and I got quite involved in the horse-racing scene they had out there. We would go down to the various stables at six in the morning and all the stable lads and trainers would tell us their tips before we headed down later in the day to watch them at the racetrack. I can't say we made much money out of our inside information, but it was good fun.

We also managed to squeeze in a lot of golf while we were there. During one game, it was Roy Saunders and me playing against Ivor and Lenny Allchurch, and we were playing for two quid a hole – not a sum to be sniffed at back then. I smashed a ball straight into the edge of a river, so Roy Saunders decided to put the pressure on me and said: 'Two quid is a lot of money and we're not wanting to lose this hole, Mel.' I said to him: 'I'll have to take it out Roy, I can't possibly play that ball – it's in the bloody river!' But he wasn't having it; he didn't want us to lose a stroke. It was just sitting at the edge, so Roy had a close look and he said: 'Mel, you'll be able to play it, there's a rock there you can use for balance. Stick your left foot on that and hook it out.' So like a fool, and not wanting to lose the two quid either, I said: 'Go on then' and gave it a bash. It might have worked, too, except that the rock was not a rock – it was only a bloody turtle, wasn't it? I went slipping and splashing into the river, the trampled turtle scuttling off as fast as its little legs would carry it, and we ended up losing the game! I'd never seen anything like it. The Allchurch brothers were rolling about the green laughing at me floundering in the water next to the turtle I'd just trodden on.

That brought back memories of another golfing gaffe I witnessed when I was playing for Arsenal. I was having a game with George Eastham and every Wednesday we would go to Dai Rees's golf course in London and take each other on. George smacked a cracker right down the middle of the course and was pleased as punch while I was muttering, 'You lucky bastard!' under my breath like the true sportsman I was. But as we were walking up the fairway to play our next shot, a big crow came swooping down and was away with George's ball in its mouth. I couldn't stand up for laughing and I think I beat him that time, thanks to my feathered friend and his timely piece of thieving.

After Mauritius and the collapse of my potato business, I lost a bit of confidence and had some tough times. I knew I wasn't cut out for trying to run my own business and there were occasions when I found myself wondering what the future held. Thankfully, I always had a lot of friends and family around me, and I still had my son Jeremy and daughter Catherine to focus on. Jeremy's football career gave me a new lease of life and I always tried to look on the bright side.

The Charles family just couldn't stay away from football – it was in our blood – and John and I took part in a lot of exhibition games for charity. I remember the two generations of the Charles family – John, Jeremy and me – all played together in a charity game in 1975 at Narbeth. The Charles name was still a big draw and we also played alongside Sir Stanley Matthews in a lot of those matches. Stan took me everywhere with him; he just wanted to keep playing on and on, and always got so much pleasure out of football. I remember we went to his 80th birthday party at Stoke and we were all presented with china plates to mark the occasion. Stan was a great guy – one of the best football has seen.

Like me, John went into business a few times and he had a big hotel in Leeds, but that didn't work out too well. He had his share of misfortune when it came to trying to make a living, but neither of us had been educated to run businesses – you've got to be the right type of bloke to run a business, haven't you? John would leave things to everyone else, and if you do that and take your eye off the ball in any way in a business, sometimes you find things are getting out of control. For him, that's exactly what happened. A few of his business ventures, including the hotel and his sports shops in Cardiff, ran into trouble and went bust. But John was still in great spirits, and wherever we went together, everyone still knew him and wanted to shake his hand.

We started seeing a lot more of each other after football and made up for the lost time. I went up to Leeds to live there next to John for four years. At the time, I was the carpet cleaner in the hotel for him, although that's probably too grand a title for what I actually did. Every morning I'd pick up the Hoover, and run it around a bit – it kept him happy, mind you, his little brother mucking in, even if it was in a small way. I also went to quite a few Leeds United games with John and his good mate Harold Williams. He was John's minder, even if he was only little. He'd been a nippy left winger in his day and was another one of the 'Buckley Boys'. Harold had set up a hell of a lot of goals for John by planting crosses from the wing on to his head. He started off with Newport County and when they knocked Leeds out the cup in 1949, Leeds said: 'We'll have your player' and signed him!

It wasn't just Leeds where I lived: I had quite a long stay in Oxford too, and after my marriage finished, I lived a bit of a nomadic existence. I've lived here, there and every-bloody-where, to be honest – I was like a Romany for a while. But no matter where I lived, I was always going to come back to Swansea in the end to spend the rest of my life there. I had my rough times, too, and it changes the way you are – I'm a totally different fellow now. Years ago there were spells when I was simply trying to find somewhere to live and to keep everything together. You get to a stage where you realise that the money's not there for you any more and you no longer have your football to keep you occupied. There's a feeling of emptiness and you really do start to fret about your future.

I came to a situation in my life where I felt that nothing seemed to be going my way and it was a struggle shaking off that feeling and trying to get my life back on track. Nothing went right for me initially because I wasn't business-minded. Sometimes people were buying off me and dealing with me because I was Mel Charles the footballer, not because I had a particularly sharp business brain. The potato business, the chicken business, all of them – one way or another they got buggered up in the end. I was fortunate in football, but out of it… I think I had used up all my good fortune. But, as I must stress, I have no regrets. What I missed out on as a kid I made up for in football because there are a lot of people who have not been lucky enough to have been where I've been. I've had a marvellous life and I'm thankful for it.

If there were any business brains in the family, they were not dished out to me. My brother Malcolm has done very well with his computer business and he always has been the sharpest of us, while my son Jeremy is doing well with his business, a sports event management company. But like I say, I've got absolutely no regrets. I might have tried and failed at a lot of things after football, but it was all part of living life to the full.

CHAPTER 20
LIKE FATHER, LIKE SON

'Jeremy was developing into a really good player, I'm not just saying that because he was my boy, and he would have made the grade regardless of the Charles name.'
MEL CHARLES

It was frustrating not being able to play anymore, and hard to finally accept that my playing days were at an end and all the trappings that came with it were over, but watching my boy Jeremy play for the Swans and Wales gave me a lot of pleasure. They were Swansea City by then, of course – they changed their name in 1970 when Swansea was granted city status, and I was delighted when Jeremy took my advice and knocked back other clubs to stay at home.

We always got on really well together and he was prepared to listen to me when he had the chance at an early age to leave Wales and go and sign for one of the big clubs in England. I took him to more or less all the big clubs – Liverpool, Manchester United and a few others. I think they were all drawn by the Charles name – the son of Mel and the nephew of John. But for all that they made him attractive offers and promised to look after him, I told him he would be best to stay at the Vetch Field and learn the game, with the security of living in his home town. I had experienced it myself, the temptation to go somewhere else when I went to Leeds as a kid, and that had been a disaster. I didn't want my son to fall into the same trap, and I thought if he stayed in Swansea and signed for the local club, he would be in good hands and that he would get his opportunity sooner rather than later.

I wasn't presenting him with a fait accompli, I was happy for him to make up his own mind, but I would have been failing in my duty as a father if I hadn't passed on the experience I had. He was a good kid and happy to listen to the advice he was getting, and so he joined the ground staff at Swansea when Harry Griffiths was the manager.

The Swans had been going through some of the toughest times in their history and when they finished third from bottom of the Fourth Division in 1975, they had to go cap-in-hand to the Football League and apply for re-election. That was a nervous time for everybody at the Vetch, because you never know if there's going to be a bit of anti-Welsh feeling bubbling underneath among the clubs from England. The club had to send a begging letter to the 91 other clubs in the league before the crunch meeting in London, and if those pleas had fallen on deaf ears then Swansea were finished. Thankfully, the other clubs gave Swansea a sympathetic hearing, voted them back in, and so the club lived on to fight another day. That decision had a big effect on Jeremy's career, because if they had been kicked out of the Football League then he would have effectively been at a dead-end club and there is no way his career would have prospered in the way that it eventually did. It was also one of the big turning points in Swansea's history, because nobody could have envisaged the amazing run of success a couple of years in the future that lifted the club to the dizziest heights it had ever occupied.

Jeremy was developing into a really good player. I'm not just saying that because he was my boy – he would have made the grade regardless of the Charles name. He was tall and had the same physique as John and me, and had a good spring in the air, which was something of a family trait and made him good at heading the ball. For John it was a gift – his ability to head a ball was amazing. People talk about him heading in goals from 30 or 40 yards and clearing the ball for 50 yards with his head when he was playing in defence, and that's no exaggeration. But I have to confess that there was somebody I considered better than John in the air. It was a guy called Pat Terry, who played for the Swan. He was fantastic in the air, probably the best I've ever seen. Pat wasn't at the Swans all that long, but he scored 9 goals in 17 games. I think even John might have conceded that he was second to him in the air.

John was in charge of the Swansea youth team at the time Jeremy was starting out, having had spells at Hereford and as manager at Merthyr Tydfil, and a lot of the young guys were responding well to his coaching. Already there were some Swansea legends-in-the-making playing in the first team – Alan Curtis, who was already a Welsh international despite playing in the Fourth Division, and Robbie James who was just a couple of years older then Jeremy. The club managed to steady themselves in 1976 after flirting with disaster the previous year, and Jeremy as a 16-year-old had helped the reserves win the Welsh League Championship too, so the foundations were being laid for some long overdue good times.

Jeremy came on as a sub against Newport County in the first match of the 1976/77 season, a League Cup tie, to make his debut at 16 and scored twice in a 4-1 win. That gave him a lot of extra confidence and I was beaming with pride as I watched him scoring in his very first game for the first team – he only took two minutes to find the net after coming off the bench. What a start!

They mostly kept Jeremy for the cup games to begin with, and used the more experienced guys in the league, but he was banging in the goals whenever his chance came. He scored a few more in the Welsh Cup and he never looked out of his depth. He was big for his age, and at 16 you just want to go out there and run about daft. By the end of the season the Swans were flying and they just missed out on promotion on the last day, despite beating the Fourth Division champions Cambridge in the final match. It had been a close-run thing, but Harry Griffiths had sowed the seeds for success and Jeremy was part of that – by the end of that season, his first in the big team, he was the club's top scorer with 23 goals under his belt.

Inevitably, the vultures were starting to circle and it didn't take long before I was looking round the stand at the Vetch and seeing that there were scouts from clubs in the First and Second Division hoping to snap up the new generation of Swansea talent. History was repeating itself. Just as the club had done in the Fifties, when they put up little resistance in selling me, Ivor Allchurch, Cliff Jones and Terry Medwin, now they were being confronted with exactly the same dilemma again. No sooner had the Swans found themselves with a promising bunch of young kids coming up through the ranks and promising a bright future, than the rumours were circulating that they would be sold on for a fast buck. Thankfully the Swansea board of the Seventies had a lot more resilience and foresight than they had back in the Fifties, and Jeremy and the other up-and-coming youngsters were going nowhere. A number of bids came in for him, Robbie and Alan Curtis, but they were knocked back, much to the delight and relief of the supporters.

Because they had come so close to promotion the previous season, the Swans were hot favourites to go up when the 1977/78 season kicked off, but after an up-and-down start, Harry Griffiths resigned. The fans were up in arms and people power helped persuade him to come back into the job. But when Harry came back, he was already leaning on the board to get somebody else in, and it was to prove a stroke of genius as far as Swansea's future was concerned. They managed to lure John Toshack down from Liverpool as player-manager, and with Harry as his assistant it was the start of a special time for the club. 'The potential at Swansea is immense,' said Toshack. 'I believe I have come to the right place at the right time.' He hit the nail on the head there!

But while Tosh had an immediate impact by quickly improving gates and results, there was devastating news for the club when Harry collapsed and died before a game at the Vetch, towards the end of the season against Scunthorpe. Give the players their due, they still went out there and played the match, despite their obvious grief, and won it 3–1 for Harry. There was no stopping the Swans, and driven by his memory, they went on and beat Halifax in the last game of the season at an emotional Vetch to make sure they were going up. They were out of the Fourth Division again, so it was onwards and upwards.

Terry Medwin came back to the Vetch as assistant to Toshack and Jeremy was part of an exciting team that was going to go and do some wonderful things. The one game that sticks in everyone's mind, and ended up in a famous Swansea song, was the League

Cup tie they had with Tottenham. This was the great Spurs side with Ossie Ardiles and Ricardo Villa in it, and when they came out of the hat against the Swans at the Vetch the whole town was buzzing with anticipation. The crowds were getting back to something like they had been when I was playing and there were 25,000 in there, me included, to watch the game. It was a fantastic match and when it finished 2-2, everyone was tipping Spurs to make no mistake in the replay at White Hart Lane. But amazingly, led by Toshack – who had dropped back to playing centre-half by then – the Swans pulled off one of the greatest wins in their history and beat them 3-1. The manager had good contacts and was bringing in quite a few of his ex-Liverpool mates, guys like Tommy Smith and Ian Callaghan. Jeremy knocked in 12 goals that season and Swansea made it two promotions out of two to get back into the Second Division, 14 years since they had last been so high in the league.

The advice I had given Jeremy at the outset was now paying off handsomely. He was already a Second Division player and he was getting to play alongside some really experienced guys who were jumping at the chance to join Toshack at a club that was going places. They found that first season in the Second Division quite tricky and finished mid-table, but they learnt a few lessons along the way and used that knowledge the next year to get themselves up to the promised land of the First Division. Alan Curtis was sold to Leeds, but then bought back again and that was probably the boost that they needed to make the leap.

It was great when they finally won promotion. They needed to beat Preston at Deepdale to go up, and there was a massive travelling support from Swansea to see them do it. The rugby legend Gareth Edwards was there to lend his support, but Toshack pulled a masterstroke by getting Bill Shankly to go into the dressing room beforehand. He gave them a few well-chosen words of inspiration, cracked a few jokes and blew away their nerves. It did the trick because they won convincingly 3-1. Leighton James and Tommy Craig scored the first two, with Jeremy scoring the third, a great effort into the top corner from 20 yards. There was something poetic about the goal, because there were three local Swansea lads involved in the build-up – Jeremy, Robbie James and Alan Curtis.

All the players had a big celebration at a hotel in Liverpool afterwards, with Bill Shankly there to offer his congratulations to Jeremy and his team-mates. I don't think they made it back until about two in the morning but there were still Swans fans there to greet them and get the drinks in. The Swans were going up and had succeeded where we had failed – the club was into the First Division for the first time since it had been formed in 1912.

After scoring the final goal in the Second Division the previous season, Jeremy also had the honour of scoring the club's first goal in a First Division game – the first of five as the Swans beat Leeds 5-1. Everyone was a bit stunned. We had spent that long getting to the First Division and then we won at a canter in our very first game. The Swans got to the top of the league briefly for a while in the first season in the First Division, but there was bad news for Jeremy – just like his old man, he damaged his cartilage in a game against Brighton and needed an operation. He was back reasonably quickly though and thankfully he didn't have as much bad luck as I had done with injuries.

Because he was settled, Jeremy's career flourished at Swansea and he played his part in what was a hell of a good team. Under the guidance of John Toshack they had risen from the Fourth Division to the top of the old First Division. It was the most successful run in the club's history. I was there in the stand to watch him for almost every game at the Vetch, and watching him made me so proud. Don't get me wrong, there were games where I was fidgeting uncomfortably in my seat if he was having a bad game and the crowd were giving him a hard time, but you soon learn to develop a thick skin against that kind of thing. The fans pay their money and they feel they are entitled to have their say, so it wasn't my place to be getting all upset if they were dishing it out to Jeremy. Mind you, I have to say, that hardly ever happened – he was a big favourite of the fans and he rarely had a bad game. They appreciated him because he was one of those players who gave his absolute all for the jersey and he also had a bit of character about him. He had inherited the Charles family trait of being able to play at centre-forward or centre-half and he made me very proud.

Jeremy had scored 53 goals in 247 league games for the Swans, and had won a few Welsh Cup medals before he moved on to Queen's Park Rangers in November 1983. He then signed for Oxford United in February 1985. They were being backed by Robert Maxwell's money, while he still had some anyway, and they had quite a side, with John Aldridge one of their main men. They made it to the League Cup final, or Milk Cup final as it was then, against his old club QPR in 1986 and I was so proud to see my boy out there on the pitch at Wembley, in front of 90,000, playing in a major cup final, something that I had never had the privilege to do. It was quite an occasion, and Oxford sailed through the game, winning 3-0. Trevor Hebberd and Ray Houghton scored for Oxford, before Jeremy scored to put the icing on the cake.

Jeremy really settled well in Oxford and still lives in the area, and for a while I went to live there too. I used to stay in Woodstock, near to where Churchill was born at Blenheim

Palace, and made a great friend in Keith Vickers, who ran a hotel and restaurant there. He had been a player himself with clubs like Portsmouth, West Brom and Oxford, but was a real success as a businessman and he was a smashing fellow and a real character. At one stage, he had been considering putting money into the Swans, along with Len O'Driscoll and Mel Nurse. But first Len O'Driscoll was killed in a road accident, and then Keith collapsed and died of a heart attack chasing after somebody who had been causing trouble in one of his restaurants. He was only 63 and his death left us devastated. Injuries eventually forced Jeremy to hang up the boots, but he stayed on in Oxford to do some coaching and he also coached at the Swans and Southampton.

Jeremy's international career also gave me a lot of pride. He was playing in probably the best Wales team since my generation, too. When he first broke into the team, he was playing alongside Terry Yorath, Joey Jones, Leighton Phillips, Leighton James and Bryan Flynn, with Dai Davies in goals, then later in his career the team boasted guys like Mickey Thomas, Ian Rush, Mark Hughes and Neville Southall. Jeremy scored his one and only goal for Wales against Bulgaria in a European Championship qualifier against Bulgaria at the Racecourse Ground in Wrexham in April 1983, almost 40 years after I had been kicked off the same pitch by Austria. He also got a chance to play against Brazil as I had done, this time in a friendly at Ninian Park in June 1983 and they did okay, holding them to a 1-1 draw. There was no Pelé around to break their hearts! Jeremy's final appearance for Wales was away to Finland in September 1986, a European qualifier that ended in a 1-1 draw, but by that time he had won 19 caps, which added to my 31 makes it a nice round 50 for father and son.

CHAPTER 21

FROM VETCH TO LIBERTY

'We get invited to the Liberty as guests of Swansea and they look after you very well, but give me the Vetch any day.'
Mel Charles

I HAVE LIVED MY LIFE to the full and can look back with great happiness on what I've seen and done. I've also got two marvellous children, Jeremy and Catherine, who are both big and beautiful and give me enormous pride. But I must admit, I watch football today and I can't help but wonder what might have been had John and I been playing now. Obviously, the money when we played is nothing like it is today – it makes my eyes water just trying to imagine being paid a hundred and fifty grand a week, like some of them are now, but I think I might have been happy to at least give that a try! I certainly wish I was playing now. It is mind boggling in many ways: if I was the biggest transfer fee paid between two British Clubs in 1959, how would that translate in today's money? It's frightening the way the game has gone. When

I first went to Arsenal, I was on twenty quid a week, four pounds extra for a win and two pounds for a draw. Today's wages are almost obscene, and most Premier League players will never have to worry about going short later in their lives.

I do think most of them lead a pampered existence and a lot of them should maybe read up on their football history, from my generation and other eras, to see just how good they have it. Guys like George Eastham and Jimmy Hill helped give power to the players and paved the way for them to be paid fair wages, but even they must be absolutely astonished by the vast amounts of cash in football now. How can anybody be worth £150,000 a week? The answer is they can't, but the big clubs and the television money that they rake in have made the seemingly impossible possible. I may have played football in the wrong era as far as making a few quid goes, but I have no regrets. I reckon there were more characters around in our era, and I think just writing this book and rattling off some of the names from yesteryear clearly demonstrates that.

That's not to say there are not some great players around today. The player that has undoubtedly excited me most in recent years is Cristiano Ronaldo, although he still needs to grow up a bit and get rid of all the childish theatrics that accompany his game. His ability is unquestionable though, and he is a fabulous athlete. I don't think he would have lasted too long back in the 1950s, mind you, but in today's game he must be the best player in the world. It's great that British football fans have been able to see him up close. What I always wonder is how he would have fared with the old, heavy, leather footballs that we used. The balls they use now are like balloons in comparison, and I don't think he would have managed to bend one of the old leather ones in from 40 yards somehow.

Whereas the best players seen in the Football League in the Fifties, Sixties and Seventies were all basically home internationals, the supporters of today are seeing Brazilians, Argentines, Spanish players and so on. There probably isn't a country left on the planet that hasn't provided at least one player in the Premier League. The number of foreign players in the Premier League and Football League is unbelievable now. You could count on one hand the number of players from outside the UK who played in my day, and while the imports have brought a lot of talent and excitement to our game, I don't think they should be playing here simply for the sake of it. I think it's always important to tried and develop local talent, and that's probably why the team that excites me the most at the moment is Aston Villa. They have young, home-grown players like Ashley Young and Gabriel Agbonlahor, who have been given a chance in the first team at an early age and have prospered because of it.

Although I don't go along to that many games now, I still follow football closely and it was fantastic to watch Cardiff reach the FA Cup final in 2008 – and also to see the Swans doing so well too.

It was a really sad day when Swansea left the Vetch in 2005 to move to the Liberty Stadium at Morfa. The new stadium is nice, but the Vetch is where all my memories were, and I live just a few yards over the road from the old ground now. It's just being left to rot – nothing's happened to it since they locked it up, except the grass is about ten foot high now, although plans are in place to finally redevelop the stadium and turn it into houses. They're talking about including a permanent memorial to the Vetch when the houses finally go up, and that's a nice gesture, I suppose. There was a time, after I had finished playing, when I never used to miss a game at the Vetch. The atmosphere up at the Liberty doesn't come close. We used to have a drink whenever the Swans were playing at the Vetch at the Harry Griffiths Bar. We'd congregate there at the same time every Saturday and had our own little routine. It was a unique ground to me, and when it comes down it will be a really sad day for me. I think I'll head down to the boozer with a black armband on!

I was at the famous game at the Vetch in 2003 when the Swans beat Hull City to fight off relegation in the last game of the season and keep their place in the Football League. Brian Flynn was in charge then and if the tension wasn't already bad enough, Hull went 2-1 up to put everyone through even more torture. I remember they played the tune from *The Great Escape* over the loudspeakers and that's what it was – an amazing escape. But it put the Swans back on the road to the good times and if they hadn't won that day, then they wouldn't be in the position they are now. It was such an emotional day. It would have broken my heart to see Swansea drop into the Conference – I think it would probably have been the beginning of the end.

I go to the Liberty Stadium now and again but the atmosphere is not a patch on what you used to get at the Vetch and I'm sure a lot of Swansea City fans will agree with that. I would probably go along more often, but I'm not as young as I used to be and these new stadiums are not designed for old timers like me. I can get a bit self-conscious trying to negotiate the steep steps with my sore knees, and I don't like drawing attention to myself when people see me limping. I suppose I'm a proud man, and I just don't like people fussing over me. I do have problems with the pain in my knees most days, and I have got that used to rolling bandages I could probably do it blindfold! There's nothing particularly exciting about the new stadium: none of the bars have any character and they are not shy the prices they charge either. While we do get invited to the Liberty as guests of the club from time to time, and they look after you very well, give me the Vetch any day.

I must admit that most of the Swansea matches I've been to in the past couple of years I've enjoyed, and under Roberto Martinez the style of football has been entertaining to watch. I'd still like to see more local lads making a name for themselves at Swansea. They seem to be few and far between now, and I don't think it's a case that the talent isn't out there, I just think that maybe they don't get the same opportunities. I don't want to keep harping back to our era, because I know there are massive differences, but our Swansea side was strong as a unit because we all came from the same area. It may be a pipe dream to think that it would happen again, but throwing a few more local lads into the mix would be good for the future of the club and would go down very well with the supporters.

As well as taking an active interest in football, I enjoy a little flutter on the horses from time to time. Nothing serious really, usually just a little bet at the big meetings on the Saturday and maybe on the Cheltenham Festival and the Grand National. I've got a regular weekly card school on the go at the Badminton in Sandfields, which is always good fun, and I usually pop in there to watch the big weekend matches on TV. There never seems to be any problem filling my time; I've got plenty to keep me busy and out of trouble, and my daughter Catherine works nearby so she's always able to drop in for a cup of tea and a chat.

I still see Cliff Jones from time to time when he comes down to Swansea from his home in London and I'm good pals with Mel Nurse. Terry Medwin meets up with us too and it's nice to catch up and share the old stories together. They're all lovely people and between us we've got a few tales stored in the memory bank. We all usually meet up in Mel Nurse's hotel, the Sea Haven on Oystermouth Road.

The Welsh FA have been very good at looking after their

former players over the years and we had a lot of publicity in 2008 to mark the 50th anniversary of our heroics at the 1958 World Cup. The irony was that we got one hundred times more publicity this time around than we did back then. We all did newspaper articles and television interviews, and the amount of public interest was staggering. I think the fact that we are the only Wales team to have made it to the finals has given us a special place in the hearts of the Welsh people.

There was another proud moment for the survivors of 1958 when the Welsh FA invited us to be guests of honour at the Wales v Georgia international at the Liberty on 21 August 2008. Seven of the squad from the finals in Sweden were there – myself, Ken Jones, Cliff Jones, Terry Medwin, Mel Hopkins, Stuart Williams and Colin Baker – and all of us felt touched when we were paraded on the pitch at half-time. It did cross my mind that John would be proud to see me standing there and again there was a moment when I could sense he was with us as we waved to the crowd, 50 years after we had been out there at the World Cup together. We were proud Welshmen back in 1958 and we are proud Welshman now. Wales lost the match to Georgia 2-1 after conceding an injury-time goal and that is typical of the country's luck in the decades since I wore the shirt. There have been so many near-things that it's become infuriating. It's a real shame that the likes of Ryan Giggs, Ian Rush and Mark Hughes and countless other brilliant Welsh internationals were denied the chance to play at the World Cup finals. We deserve a change of luck, and I hope and I pray that another batch of Wales players will soon follow in our footsteps to the World Cup finals. If they do ever make it there again at least they won't have Pelé to spoil their party!

STATISTICS

INTERNATIONAL CAPS: 31 INTERNATIONAL GOALS: 6

1955
20 APRIL
Northern Ireland (Windsor Park, Belfast)
3–2 (J. Charles hat-trick)
23 NOVEMBER
Austria (Racecourse Ground, Wrexham)
1–2 (Tapscott)
1956
20 OCTOBER
Scotland (Ninian Park, Cardiff)
2–2 (Ford, Medwin)
14 NOVEMBER
England (Wembley, London)
1–3 (J. Charles)

1957

10 APRIL

Northern Ireland (Windsor Park, Belfast)

0–0

1 MAY

Czechoslovakia (Ninian Park, Cardiff)

1–0 (Vernon)

19 MAY

East Germany (Zentralstadion, Leipzig)

1–2 (M. Charles)

26 MAY

Czechoslovakia (Stadion Juliska, Prague)

0–2

25 SEPTEMBER

East Germany (Ninian Park, Cardiff)

4–1 (Palmer hat-trick, C. Jones)

19 OCTOBER

England (Ninian Park, Cardiff)

0–4

1958

15 JANUARY

Israel (Ramat Gan Stadium, Tel Aviv)

2–0 (I. Allchurch, Bowen)

5 FEBRUARY

Israel (Ninian Park, Cardiff)

2–0 (I. Allchurch, C. Jones)

8 JUNE

Hungary (Jernvallen, Sanviken)

1–1 (J. Charles)

11 JUNE
Mexico (Rasunda Stadium, Stockholm)
1–1 (I. Allchurch)
15 JUNE
Sweden (Rasunda Stadium, Stockholm)
0–0
17 JUNE
Hungary (Rasunda Stadium, Stockholm)
2–1 (I. Allchurch, Medwin)
19 JUNE
Brazil (Nya Ullevi Stadion, Gothenburg)
0–1
18 OCTOBER
Scotland (Ninian Park, Cardiff)
0–3
26 NOVEMBER
England (Villa Park, Birmingham)
2–2 (Tapscott, I. Allchurch)
1959
4 NOVEMBER
Scotland (Hampden Park, Glasgow)
1–1 (J. Charles)
1961
12 APRIL
Northern Ireland (Windsor Park, Belfast)
5–1 (M. Charles, C. Jones 2, I Allchurch, Leek)
19 APRIL
Spain (Ninian Park, Cardiff)
1–2 (Woosnam)

18 MAY

Spain (Madrid)

1-1 (I. Allchurch)

28 MAY

Hungary (Budapest)

2-3 (I. Allchurch, C. Jones)

8 NOVEMBER

Scotland (Hampden)

0-2

1962

11 APRIL

Northern Ireland (Ninian Park, Cardiff)

4-0 (M. Charles 4)

12 MAY

Brazil (Maracana, Rio de Janeiro)

1-3 (I. Allchurch)

16 MAY

Brazil (Sao Paulo)

1-3 (Leek)

22 MAY

Mexico (Mexico City)

1-2 (J. Charles)

20 OCTOBER

Scotland (Ninian Park, Cardiff)

2-3 (I. Allchurch, J. Charles)

1963

20 MARCH

Hungary (Ninian Park, Cardiff)

1-1 (C. Jones pen)

CLUB STATISTICS

Football League
Swansea Town (1952 –1959): 233 appearances, 69 goals
Arsenal (1959 –1962): 60 appearances, 26 goals
Cardiff City (1962 –1965): 81 appearances, 24 goals
Port Vale (1966 –1967): 7 appearances, 0 goals

Other clubs played for
Porthmadog (1965 –1966)
Oswestry Town (1967)
Haverfordwest (1967–1972)

FINISHING LEAGUE POSITIONS

PORT VALE

Season	Div	Pld	W	D	L	F	A	Pts	Position
1966–67	Div 4	46	14	15	17	55	58	43	13th

CARDIFF CITY

1964–65	Div 2	42	13	14	15	64	57	40	13th
1963–64	Div 2	42	14	10	18	56	81	38	15th
1962–63	Div 2	42	18	7	17	83	73	43	10th
1961–62	Div 1	42	9	14	19	50	81	32	21st (RELEGATED)

ARSENAL

1961–62	Div 1	42	16	11	15	71	72	43	10th
1960–61	Div 1	42	15	11	16	77	85	41	11th
1959–60	Div 1	42	15	9	18	68	80	39	13th
1958–59	Div 1	42	21	8	13	88	68	50	3rd

SWANSEA TOWN

1958–59	Div 2	42	16	9	17	79	81	41	11th
1957–58	Div 2	42	11	9	22	72	99	31	19th
1956–57	Div 2	42	19	7	16	90	90	45	10th
1955–56	Div 2	42	20	6	16	83	81	46	10th
1954–55	Div 2	42	17	9	16	86	83	43	10th
1953–54	Div 2	42	13	8	21	58	82	34	20th
1952–53	Div 2	42	15	12	15	78	81	42	11th

THE WORLD CUP
SUNDAY 8 JUNE 1958 AT THE JERNVALLEN, SANDVIKEN
Hungary 1 (Bozsik 4), Wales 1 (J. Charles 26)
Hungary: Gyula Grosics, Sandor Matrái, Laszlo Sárosi, Joszef
Bozsik, Ferenc Sipos, Pal Berendi, Karoly Sándor, Nandor
Hidegkuti (captain), Lajos Tichy, Dezso Bundzsák, Mate
Fenyvesi.
Wales: Jack Kelsey, Stuart Williams, Mel Hopkins, Derek
Sullivan, Mel Charles, Dave Bowen (captain), Colin Webster,
Terry Medwin, John Charles, Ivor Allchurch, Cliff Jones.
Attendance: 15,343. Referee: Jose Maria Codesal (Uruguay)

WEDNESDAY 11 JUNE 1958 AT THE RÅSUNDA STADION, SOLNA
Mexico 1 (Belmonte 69), Wales 1 (I. Allchurch 32)
Mexico: Antonio Carbajal, Jesus Del Muro, Raul Cárdenas
(captain), Jaime Belmonte, Jorge Romo, Francisco Flóres, Carlos
González, Salvador Reyes, Carlos Blanco, Crescencio Gutiérrez,
Enrique Sesma.
Wales: Jack Kelsey, Stuart Williams, Mel Hopkins, Colin Baker,
Mel Charles, Dave Bowen (captain), Colin Webster, Terry
Medwin, John Charles, Ivor Allchurch, Cliff Jones.
Attendance: 15,000. Referee: Leo Leme?ic (Yugoslavia)

SUNDAY 15 JUNE 1958 AT THE RÅSUNDA STADION, SOLNA
Sweden 0, Wales 0
Sweden: Karl Svensson, Orvar Bergmark, Sven Axbom,
Börjesson, Bengt Gustavsson (captain), Sigvard Parling, Berndt
Berndtson, Arne Selmonsson, Henry Källgren, Gosta Löfgren,
Lennart Skoglund.
Wales: Jack Kelsey, Stuart Williams, Mel Hopkins, Derek
Sullivan, Mel Charles, Dave Bowen (captain), Roy Vernon,
Ronnie Hewitt, John Charles, Ivor Allchurch, Cliff Jones.
Attendance: 30,287. Referee: Lucien van Nuffel (Belgium)

Final group table

	Pld	W	D	L	F	A	Pts
Sweden	3	2	1	0	5	1	5
Hungary	3	1	1	1	6	3	3
Wales	3	0	3	0	3	3	3
Mexico	3	0	1	2	1	8	1

Play-off match
Tuesday 17 June 1958 at Råsunda Stadion, Solna.
Wales 2 (I Allchurch 55, Medwin 76), Hungary 1 (Tichy 33)
Wales: Jack Kelsey, Stuart Williams, Mel Hopkins, Derek
Sullivan, Mel Charles, Dave Bowen (captain), Terry Medwin,
Ron Hewitt, John Charles, Ivor Allchurch, Cliff Jones.
Hungary: Gyula Grosics (captain), Sandor Matrái, Laszlo Sárosi,
Joszef Bozsik, Ferenc Sipos, Joszef Bencsics, Antal Kotasz, Laszlo
Budai, Lajos Tichy, Dezso Bundzsák, Mate Fenyvesi.
Attendance: 2,823. Referee: Nicolai Latichev (Russia)

Quarter-final

Thursday 19 June 1958 at Nya Ullevi Stadion, Gothenburg
Brazil 1 (Pelé 73), Wales 0
Brazil: Gilmar, De Sordi, N Santos, Zito, Bellini (captain),
Orlando, Garrincha, Didi, Mazzola, Pelé, Zagalo.
Wales: Jack Kelsey, Stuart Williams, Mel Hopkins, Derek
Sullivan, Mel Charles, Dave Bowen (captain), Terry Medwin,
Ron Hewitt, Colin Webster, Ivor Allchurch, Cliff Jones.
Attendance: 25,923. Friedrich Seipelt (Austria)